TIFFIN
GLASS 1914-1940

Leslie Piña & Jerry Gallagher

Introduction by Ed Goshe

77 Lower Valley Road, Atglen, PA 19310

Printed in Hong Kong
ISBN: 0-7643-0102-0

Library of Congress Cataloging-in-Publication Data

Piña, Leslie A. , 1947-
    Tiffin glass, 1914-1940 / Leslie Piña & Jerry Gallagher: introduction by Ed. Goshe.
       p. cm.
    Includes bibliographical references and index.
    ISBN: 0-7643-0102-0 (hard)
    1. Tiffin Glass Company--Catalogs. 2. Stemware--Ohio--Tiffin--Catalogs. 3. Depression glass--Collectors and collecting--United States--Catalogs. I. Gallagher, Jerry. II. Title.
NK5198.T53A4 1996
748.29171'24--dc20   96-18906
                                         CIP

Trade journal advertisements, courtesy of Jones S.R.S. Archives and Ruth Hemminger.

Published by Schiffer Publishing, Ltd.
77 Lower Valley Road
Atglen, PA 19310
Phone: (610) 593-1777
Fax: (610) 593-2002
Please write for a free catalog.
This book may be purchased from the publisher.
Please include $2.95 for shipping.
Try your bookstore first.

We are interested in hearing from authors with book ideas on related subjects.

CONTENTS

CREDITS

Tiffin Glass 1914-1940 is an effort to classify and present information currently known about Tiffin glass. Although we have attempted to clarify some former grey areas of research and introduce previously unpublished material, there is an overwhelming realization that Tiffin Glass research is still in its infancy.

Although the Bibliography lists publications which are readily available to collectors of Tiffin glass, this work is intended as a categorical introduction and sample of Tiffin colors and shapes which were produced, between 1914 and 1940, at Factory R in Tiffin, Ohio. Many people have shared their research files and been helpful in documenting information. Many thanks for access to the Jones S.R.S. Archives as well as the Goshe and Hemminger Archives of Tiffin Glass. Hours of unstinting research assistance were generously rendered by Ed Goshe, Ruth Hemminger, Randall Supplee, Norma Jenkins and the staff of the Rakow Library at the Corning Glass Center, Corning, New York, Helen and Bob Jones, the Editorial Committee of the Tiffin Glass Collectors Club (T.G.C.C.), Aniceta Zamborsky, and staff members of the Library of Congress in Washington, D.C., and The Carnegie Library in Pittsburgh. Particularly helpful were advertisements found in *China, Glass and Lamps* and *Crockery & Glass Journal*, trade papers on deposit in the libraries listed above, as well as "Show and Tell" reports and feature articles contained in the *Tiffin Glassmasters Newsletter*, quarterly publication of T.G.C.C.

Gratitude is also expressed to the following collectors of Tiffin glass who shared and allowed hands-on study of hundreds of pieces from their collections: the Seneca County Museum of Tiffin, Ohio; John Bing, Bill Reyer, Ed Goshe, Lyman and Ruth Hemminger, Richard and Virginia Distel, Harold and Betty Scherger, Dale and Eunice Cover, Phil and Rayella Engle, Gerald Eakin, Robert and Helen Jones, Roger and Luanna Lavoie, Fran Jay and Marv Silverstein, Dennis Lockard, Philip Platten, Frank and Jean Consentino, and Roy and Cynthia Ash.

Of course, no book is possible without the help and support of the publisher and staff. Special thanks to Nancy and Peter Schiffer at Schiffer Publishing.

FOREWORD

Leslie Piña

"Tiffin Glass" has been a collaborative adventure that has included many people—even beyond the list of generous contributors who lent items to be photographed and/or provided information (see Credits). Ramón and I made many memorable trips to Tiffin, Ohio. Ramón designed and built a portable photography studio, and he was an important part of our team at each session. Ed Goshe and Ruth and Lyman Hemminger demonstrated their passion for this glass and dedication to the project, and Ramón and I remember their warm hospitality. May all of our efforts be worthy of this impressive glass company.

Although Tiffin glass was made for the better part of a century, there were four milestone dates: 1889 with the opening of the glass factory in Tiffin, Ohio (or perhaps 1892 when it joined the United States Glass Company); 1914 when the production of blown ware became the focus; 1940 with the introduction of the Swedish Line and beginning of the modern era; and finally 1980 when the furnace cooled.

We have selected the years 1914 to 1940 for this volume, because they represent a visually and stylistically coherent period. The product of these early years is primarily traditional in form (although a few exceptions of what might be called Art Deco are included). The Swedish Line, introduced in 1940, and the fifties modern freeform and biomorphic shapes are so entirely different from the earlier styles that 1940 becomes a neat and logical boundary and ending date for a book. Stemware and tableware were made throughout Tiffin's history, and earlier patterns sometimes remained in production after 1940. This makes it difficult to categorize them as being in the earlier "traditional" or the later "modern" period. We have therefore presented primarily decorative items for table and shelf. These candleholders, vases, figurals, lamps, and novelties are among the most recognizable and sought-after items of American handmade glass belonging to what is commonly referred to as the Depression Era.

Among the many attributes of Tiffin glass, perhaps color is the most striking. While the shapes and other stylistic features of the period 1914-1940, such as luxurious satin finishes, are noteworthy, color can be a real joy. Some prefer the subtle pastels in Tiffin's repertoire, while others like the intense and deeply saturated hues and the bold contrasts created by decorating silky black glass with vibrant oranges and yellows. Tiffin glass can accommodate any taste with its extraordinary variety, much of which is presented in the pages that follow. Whether a seasoned collector or a more recent admirer, Tiffin glass is sure to delight, and I hope that these pictures will motivate readers to look at the actual glass objects more carefully. Personal encounters with beauty—be they in art or in nature—are always pleasures worth searching for.

RESEARCH BACKGROUND
Jerry Gallagher

My personal interest in Tiffin Glass was awakened while I researched another titan of the glass industry, the Morgantown Glass Works of Morgantown, West Virginia. The similarity of many colors as well as some items of glassware produced by the two companies was a confusing issue for a number of years until an explanation for the similarity between certain Tiffin and Morgantown shades and shapes became apparent in the personage of George Dougherty. Dougherty was part of the management team when Factory R became the 'Tiffin Catalogue' source for glassware produced in all of the plants of the United States Glass Company conglomerate at that time. Also, in the mid-teens when the Tiffin plant was designated as the U. S. Glass Company's flagship for blown ware, Dougherty was instrumental in adding more 'color ware' to the primarily all-Crystal production of Factory R. A number of Tiffin colors which were introduced during this period eventually also appeared as Morgantown colors after Dougherty's advent to the Morgantown Glass Works in 1923, e.g. Tiffin BLUE has the same tonality as Morgantown's NANKING BLUE while Morgantown's PRIMROSE has a definite affinity to Tiffin's CANARY, both of which are known as 'vaseline glass' today. Collectors will also find similar shades in some of the other colored wares produced by the two companies. Dougherty was instrumental, too, in the development of some colors for the Libbey Glass Company of Toledo, Ohio. A serious student and patron of the arts, George Dougherty left his colorful imprint on the entire glass industry, but Tiffin and Morgantown were the most significant recipients of his artistic perception and innovative use of color during his tenures at each facility.

Research for this book has relied heavily on trade publications as well as the archival materials of Tiffin glass researchers and collectors. The factory run sheets, ledgers, and other paper memorabilia found in the Goshe and Hemminger Archives were singularly helpful in verifying color and, in some instances, pattern names. Readers will note the frequent use of italics *for emphasis* throughout the text. "Double quotation marks" indicate words or phrases which are recorded directly from trade journals as well as Tiffin company files or catalogs. Words or phrases enclosed by 'single quotation marks' signify terminology understood, accepted, and commonly used by glass collectors. Occasional photo references are used throughout the text, e.g. (3.25) translates to 'chapter three, illustration #25'.

Readers will note the use of 'Amberina' in place of Tiffin's "Red" throughout the text. Since Tiffin collectors readily accept and use the term Amberina in place of Red, we have opted for this change of color terminology to alleviate confusion between Red and Tiffin's "Ruby" which was another Tiffin color produced during the same time frame.

Measurements are listed when known. Boxes, bowls, compotes, ashtrays, and plates are measured at their widest diameter. Measurements for baskets are taken at the widest diameter of the flared rim, not the height of the basket. Height, however, is listed for candleholders, Tiffin and USGC Crests, jugs, lamps, and figurals. When measuring diameters or heights, there can be a variance of as much as 1/2 inch between identical pieces in a Line.

Values given at the end of each caption are listed in the order in which the items are shown in the accompanying illustration. Range of value, of course, is based on a number of factors, not the least being the variance of prices reported in shops and at shows throughout the country. The price ranges listed represent actual purchase prices. Availability and/or rarity also affect prices. Readers will find no values listed for true rarities or those Lines which are as yet not fully documented. Nor is it possible to give a range of value for offhand work, such as the epergne (8.35) and the group of miniatures attributed to Victor Hendrix (8.36), since those items were unique non-production efforts which were never offered for sale through Tiffin retail outlets.

Although every effort was made to avoid mistakes, research is full of surprises and one does well to remember that "The role of research is not only to build on what we have already learned but to also unlearn what we have erroneously thought we knew to be fact when it wasn't fact at all!"

There are between 25,000 and 30,000 pieces of glassware in the new show rooms in the Pottery and Glass Building, 954 Liberty Avenue in Pittsburgh, Pennsylvania. The art glass lines, such as the colored and decorated glass, have been placed in the front of the display room. The high class blown and stemware lines are in the eight booths on the east side of the big room. Then, in the southwest corner of the room, the lighting line has been displayed, and this is a most attractive corner. Several new items have been added to this line within the last few weeks, and since the close of the annual Pottery and Glass Exposition.

"In the center of the room, display tables have been placed, upon which have been placed such items as console sets, vases, flower bowls and such similar items, both in plain and colored glass. A special room has been provided where the various lines of plain tumblers, goblets, jugs and nappies are being shown. In all, 40 tables are used for display purposes in addition to the shelving and tables in the eight sidewall booths." (*Crockery and Glass Journal*, March 13, 1924, pp. 20 & 21).

Introduction
THE HISTORY AND COLORS OF TIFFIN GLASS

Ed Goshe

The A. J. Beatty and Sons Glass Factory began production in Tiffin, Ohio, primarily as a pressed tumbler operation, on August 15, 1889. The factory joined the United States Glass Company conglomerate on January 1, 1892, and was known thereafter as Factory R. The facility continued as a pressed tumbler operation until 1897, at which time the pressed ware department was moved to Gas City, Indiana.

By 1914, the focus of production at Factory R was on blown ware. Becoming well known for their cut crystal lines, the reputation of Tiffin cuttings was exploited by the parent company in national advertising campaigns. By the mid-1920s, Factory R became the flagship factory of the United States Glass Company. In 1927 the United States Glass Company's famous shield crest label was altered by the removal of the "USGC" logo from the center of the shield and the insertion of "TIFFIN" superimposed over a large "T" (*Crockery and Glass Journal*, September 27, 1927). Glassware produced at the other plants in the conglomerate was also included in the TIFFIN Catalogs. The identification of USGC products as TIFFIN GLASS was now complete.

In the mid-1920s, glass buyers wanted new hues to enhance their homes, and the Tiffin plant helped fill this niche by introducing many new colors. The Tiffin spectrum included: Black; Blue, a medium shade frequently used in combination with Canary; Sky Blue, pastel azure; Canary, Tiffin's vaseline; Jasper, blue with green overtones; Reflex Green, pastel "light green"; Emerald Green, a true green; Ruby, deep tonality; Amberina, Tiffin's "Red" shading to areas of orange and yellow; Amber,

a brown complexion; Lilac, a pale lavender; Amethyst, a medium deep purple; Rose Pink, a medium soft blush found at times with an orange cast; Opal, 'milk' white; Old Gold, amber toned yellow which fluoresces to tangerine under black light; Twilite, an amethyst hued blue also identified as Tiffin's "evening blue"; Royal Blue, a true deep cobalt; Ivory, 'white' opaque with a grey cast; Nile Green, as seen in the reeded stem of the #15016. Line; and Mandarin Yellow, Tiffin's pale topaz. Ruby, Jasper, Lilac, and Ivory are rare while Twilite and Royal Blue are considered scarce.

Although the company is famous today for their production colors, crystal was always the main output at Factory R. The production and sale of blown stemware, both decorated and undecorated, paid the bills at the Tiffin Glass Factory. Factory R managed to survive the Depression while many other factories in the conglomerate were being closed. In 1937, the offices of the United States Glass Company were transferred from Pittsburgh to Tiffin, and C. W. Carlson was elected president. Given the task of getting the company out of debt, he immediately liquidated several unproductive plants while new life was breathed into Factory R with Carlson's introduction of the Swedish Modern Line in 1940. Additional lines of innovative glassware were developed and produced under his direction during the next two decades, and his tenure as president from 1938 to 1959 is considered by many to be the "Golden Age of Tiffin Glass."

The production of Crystal and Cobalt continued under Carlson, but he is also credited with the introduction of many new colors. Copen Blue, a 'tarnished' but brilliant medium hue, was introduced in the early 1940s. Three of today's most collectible Tiffin colors were introduced in the late 1940s and early 1950s: Killarney, dark green with a definite black tonality; Wistaria, a vibrant 'rosy red' which pales to pink in thinner portions of the glass; and Twilight, Tiffin's dichromatic lavender shade which assumes a blue tonality under fluorescent light. Dawn, which is exactly the same color formula as Twilight, was the color name for items produced from Duncan Glass molds in the late 1950s. Tiffin had acquired the old Duncan and Miller molds in 1955 and advertised the following Lines in Catolog #93 as patterns produced by the Duncan and Miller Division of the United States Glass Company at Tiffin, Ohio: #41 Early American Sandwich, #115 Canterbury, #301 Teardrop, #30 Pall Mall, #152 Patio, #127 Murano, #71 American Way, and "Duncan's White Milk Glass". Many of these Lines were offered in Tiffin production colors of that era as well as in Crystal.

The following colors were also produced in the late 1950s: Azure, a very pale blue; Cerulean, another pale blue which looks like Twilight/Dawn under fluorescent light; White Milk Glass; Plum, essentially a reintroduction of Amethyst; Golden Banana, a yellow with honey gold overtones; and Cornsilk, a soft yellow with less vibrancy than Golden Banana. Ruby was also in production at this time.

When Carlson retired in 1959, the company was struggling for survival. This prompted the head office to add additional colors to the

Tiffin spectrum: Smoke, a soft grey, was introduced in 1959; their short-lived Empire Green, an intense olive shade followed in 1961. The company filed bankruptcy in 1962 and actually closed down for a few months, but in 1963 four former employees purchased the facility and resumed production as the Tiffin Art Glass Corporation. Two colors were developed and marketed during this period: Citron, a medium yellow-green, and Desert Red, a subdued orange-brown with red overtones apparent in thicker portions of the glass.

After the plant was sold to Continental Can Company in 1966, the new owners marketed the final two shades of Tiffin Glass: Greenbriar, an avocado green used in the production of many items circa 1966, and Persimmon, a true orange shading to yellow, sometimes found with a distinct opalescence. Continental Can sold the facility to Interpace Corporation in December of 1968, and in May of 1979 the factory was purchased by Towle Silversmiths. Although the fires were allowed to die on May 1, 1980, Towle continued a cutting operation at the site and sold off inventory until October 1984, at which time the Outlet Store was closed forever.

Tiffin Glass has become increasingly popular with connoisseurs of fine American handmade glassware. Both stemware and the art glass lines continue to increase in value as more collectors and dealers come to appreciate the quality and intriguing beauty of Tiffin Glass.

Chapter One
BASKETS AND CRESTS

Collectors of fine handmade glass produced by the United States Glass Company rightfully refer to their collections as "TIFFIN Glass" regardless of the factory of origin. In a 1927 two page advertisement, the Pittsburgh-based firm not only introduced their 'altered crest' but also published their earlier decision to henceforth advertise all USGC products as "TIFFIN," named after Factory R in Tiffin, Ohio: "The world's largest makers of household glassware announce the presentation of TIFFINware to the women of America. Now, to the famous gold Shield of the world's largest makers of Household Glassware is added the familiar name 'TIFFIN,' and TIFFINware becomes in name, as for years it has been IN FACT, America's foremost line of finer quality glassware for every household use and decorative purpose." *Crockery and Glass Journal*, September 19, 1927).

1.1 - When "a new display sign" was introduced in 1925, retailers were advised, "A few of these little glass replicas of the Trade Mark of Quality should be on your display tables and shelves. They are made from fine pot glass in various colors, are about 7 inches high, and will be sent without charge upon request" (*Crockery and Glass Journal*, April 9, 1925, p. 12). U.S.G.C. 6" Shield Crest in Reflex Green Satin with gold decoration. (250-300)

1.2 - Although advertised as "about 7 inches high," U.S.G.C. Shield Crest Signs measure just over 6" in height. United States Glass Company 6" Shield Crest in Sky Blue Satin with gold decoration. (250-300)

1.3 - Tiffin 6" Shield Crest, Black with gold decoration. (275-325)

The Gold TIFFIN Crest on every piece

1.4 - Premier announcement of the U. S. Glass Company's altered Shield Crest, with "TIFFIN" replacing the "USGC" logo (*Crockery and Glass Journal*, September 27, 1927, p.19).

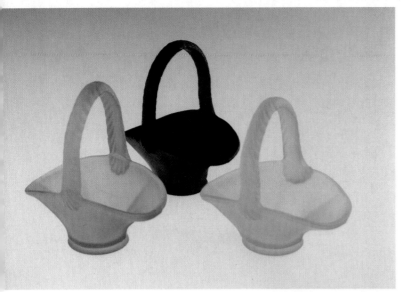

1.5 - #310. 3 1/2" Satin Glass Favor Baskets ("Serving Baskets," 1.27) in Emerald Green, Black, and Sky Blue. (30-40 each)

1.6 - #310. 3 1/2" Favor Baskets in Rose Pink, Canary, Emerald Green, Reflex Green, and Old Gold. (20-30 each)

1.7 - #310. Line in Old Gold: left, 3 1/2" Favor Basket; center, 6" Basket; right, 3-3/4" Candleholder. (25-45, 40-65, 20-30).

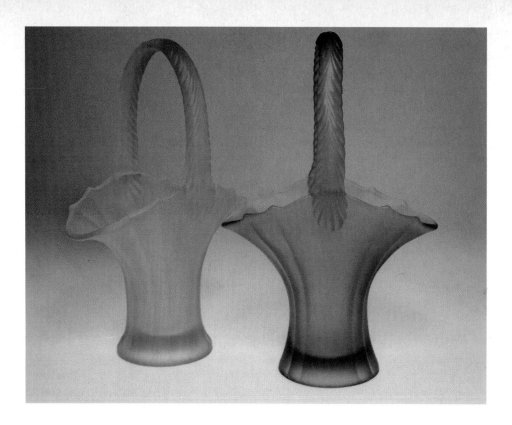

1.8 - #310. 6" Satin Glass Baskets: left, Reflex Green;
right, Emerald Green. (55-75 each)

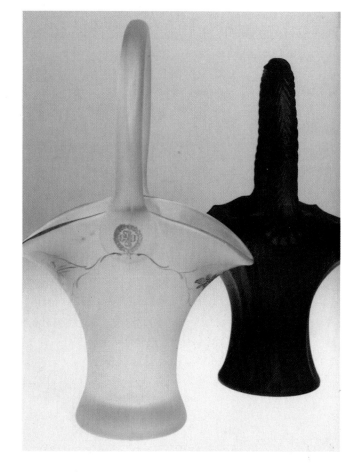

1.9 - #310. 6" Amberina Basket. (65-95).

1.10 - Left, #9574. 6" Crystal Satin Glass Basket with
gold tracery decoration; right, #310. 6" Black Satin
Glass Basket. (65-95, 50-75)

1.11 - Left, #9574. 6" Basket; right, #66. 7 1/2" Candlesticks. All in Canary. (50-75, 65-85)

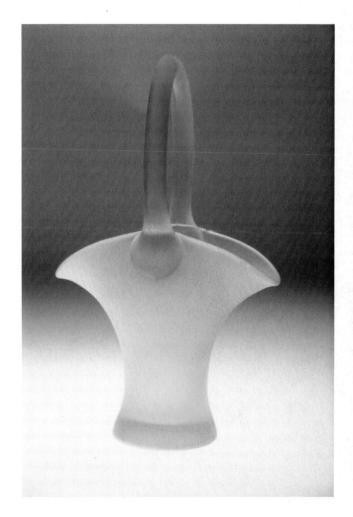

1.12 - #9574. 6" Canary Satin Glass Basket. (60-85)

1.13 - #9574. 6" Black Satin Glass Basket with gold decoration. (65-90)

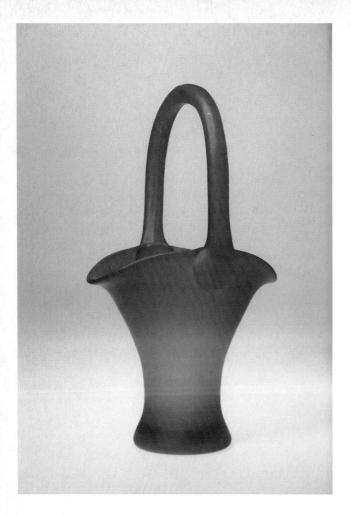

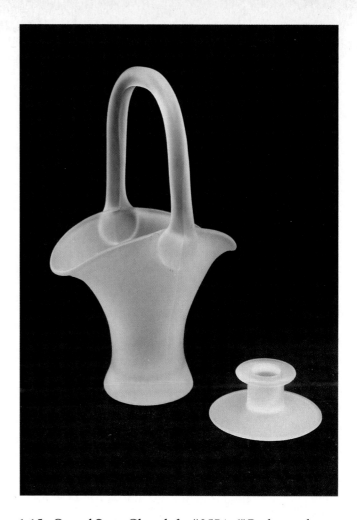

1.14 - #9574. 6" Amberina Satin Glass Basket. (50-75)

1.15 - Crystal Satin Glass: left, #9574. 6" Basket; right, #10. 3 1/2" Candleholder. (55-75, 20-25 pair)

1.16 - Black Satin Glass with gold stencil 'Ship Decoration': #9574. 6" Basket, #151. 8" Cupped Dahlia Vase, #319. 8 1/2" Oval Candy Box, and #10. 3 1/2" Candleholders, (80-100, 75-95, 95-125, 35-55)

1.17 - #9574. 6" Satin Glass Baskets: Amberina and Sky Blue. (65-75, 55-65)

1.18 - #9574. 6" Satin Glass Baskets: Emerald Green, Canary, and Crystal. (55-65, 55-65, 45-55)

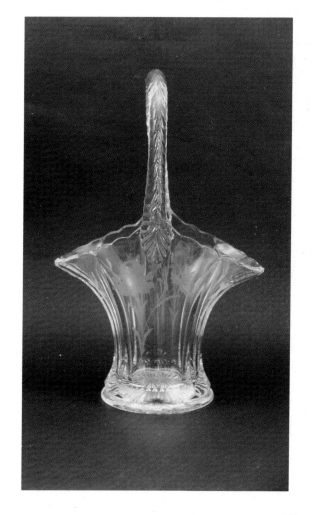

1.19 - Crystal #9583. 7" Basket with light cutting. (65-85)

1.20 - Left, #15151. 7" Sky Blue Art Basket with Crystal trim; center and right, #012. 8 1/2" Rose Pink and Sky Blue Candy Jars. (35-55, 55-75, 60-80)

1.21 - #15151. 7" Crystal Art Basket with Emerald Green trim. (30-50)

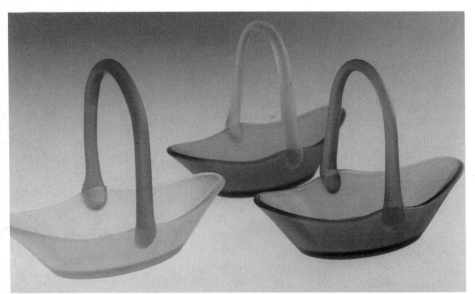

1.22 - #15151. 7" Satin Glass Art Baskets: left, Crystal with Emerald Green trim; center, Emerald Green with Crystal trim; right, Emerald Green. (40-65 each)

1.23 - #15151. 7" Satin Glass Art Baskets: left, Canary; center, Canary with Crystal trim; right, Crystal with Canary trim. (40-60 each)

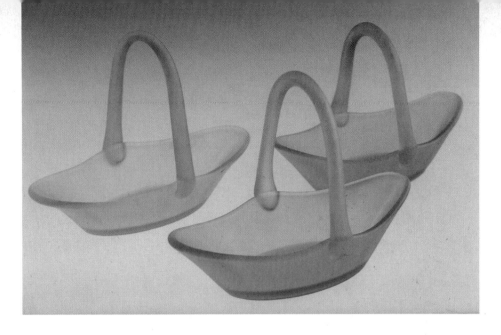

1.24 - #15151. 7" Satin Glass Art Baskets: left, Crystal with Sky Blue trim; center, Sky Blue with Crystal trim; right, Sky Blue. (40-60 each)

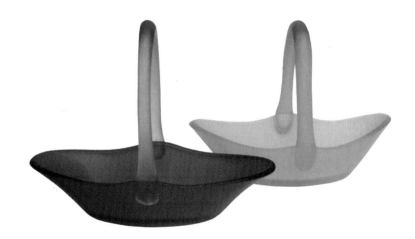

1.25 - #15151. 7" Satin Glass Art Baskets: left, Amberina with Crystal trim; right, Sky Blue. (30-50, 35-55)

1.26 - #15151. 7" Satin Glass Art Baskets: Reflex Green and Amberina. (45-60 each)

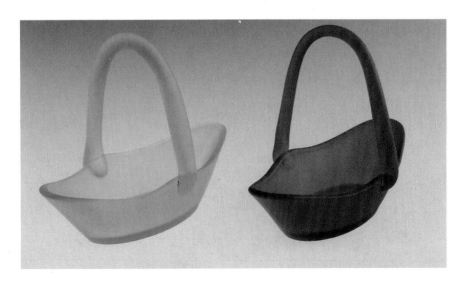

1.27 - *Crockery and Glass Journal*, November 27, 1924, p. 9.

1.28 - Old Gold #15308. 10-3/4" Basket. (135-155)

1.29 - Black Satin Glass 13" Basket, unknown Line Number. (125-150)

Chapter Two
BOWLS AND COMPOTES

2.1 - Console Set: Rose Pink Satin #179. 7" Nasturtium Bowl on Black Satin Base and #10. 3 1/2" Candleholders, fired enamel floral decoration with gold trim. (3-piece set, 125-145)

2.2 - Unknown gold encrusted etched border on Black Satin #179. 7" Nasturtium Bowl with cover and base. (95-125)

2.3 - Detail of gold encrusted etching on Black Satin #179. 7" Nasturtium Bowl.

2.4 - Silver Overlay decoration on Sky Blue Satin #179. 7" Nasturtium Bowl with undecorated Sky Blue Satin base. (135-155)

2.5 - Sky Blue Satin and Emerald Green Satin #179. 7" Nasturtium Bowls on Black Satin bases. (45-65, 40-60)

2.6 - Amberina Satin Glass and Amber Satin Glass #179. 7" Nasturtium Bowls on Black Satin bases. (45-65, 40-60)

2.7 - Emerald Green, Amberina, and Sky Blue Satin Glass #179. 7" Flower Bowls. (35-45 each)

2.8 - Amber Satin Glass: left, #15331. 11 1/2" Spiral Optic Fruit Bowl; right, #179. 9 1/2" non-optic Console Bowl. (40-55, 45-65)

2.9 - Amberina Satin Glass: left, #15179. Sweet Pea Vase; right, #179. 7 1/2" High Foot Compote. (30-45, 35-50)

2.10 - Black Satin Glass #15179. 11" Orange Bowl with gold encrusted Minton variant band. (65-75)

2.11 - Gold Line Decoration No. 1 Royal Blue Satin
#15179. Two-handled Bowls: left, 10" Console Bowl;
right, 4-3/4" Whipped Cream. (100-150, 45-65)

2.14 - Satin Glass #15179. 9" Low Foot Flared Compotes in Amberina and Black. (30-50 each)

2.12 - #15179. 10 1/2" Tourraine Ruby Satin Glass
Low Foot Compote. (150-175)

2.13 - Satin Glass #15179. 9" Low Foot Flared Compotes in Emerald Green and Canary. (35-50 each)

2.15 - Black Satin Glass #15179. 8 1/2" Flower Bowl,
with Silver Overlay and fired enamel floral decoration.
(125-175)

2.16 - Emerald Green Satin Glass #310. 11 1/2" Open Work Compote. (55-75)

2.18 - Canary and Emerald Green Satin Glass #310. 8 1/2" Open Work Compotes. (35-55 each)

2.19 - Amberina and Black Satin Glass #310. 8 1/2" Open Work Compotes. (45-65 each)

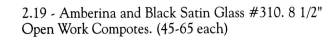

2.17 - Amberina Satin Glass #310. 11 1/2" Open Work Compote. (65-85)

2.20 - Tiffin Stretch Glass: left, #310. 6 1/2" Rose Pink Compote with fired enamel floral decoration; right, #310. 10" Amber Rolled Edge Bowl. (55-70, 25-40)

2.21 - Satin Glass #315. 7 1/2" Low Foot Compotes in Rose Pink, Canary, and Emerald Green. (40-60, 30-50, 30-50)

2.22 - Satin Glass #315. 10" Low Foot Compotes in Black and Amberina. (45-75 each)

2.23 - Satin Glass #315. 7 1/2"
High Foot Compotes in Black and
Canary. (45-65, 40-60)

2.24 - Satin Glass #315. 7 1/2"
High Foot Compotes in Emerald
Green and Amberina. (40-60, 50-
70)

2.25 - Emerald Green Satin Glass
#15315. 7 1/2" Low Foot Com-
pote. (30-45)

2.26 - Sky Blue Satin Glass #15310. 7" High Foot
Compote and #315. 7" High Foot Compote. (40-60
each)

25

2.27 - Black Satin Glass #15319. 8" Candlesticks and
10" Compote with fired enamel "Egyptian Decoration."
(185-225, set)

2.29 - Silver Overlay decoration
on #15319. 10" High Foot Compote (2.28).

2.28 - Black Satin Glass #15319. 10" High Foot Compote with Silver Overlay decoration. (155-225)

2.30 - Emerald Green Satin Glass #8076. 11" Open Work Orange Bowl and #3201. 6" High Foot Compote. (40-60, 20-35)

2.31 - Gold Line Decoration No. 1 Royal Blue Satin Glass #8098. 7 1/2" Footed Rose Bowl and base. (100-125)

2.32 - Sky Blue #8105. 9" Rolled Edge Bowl. (30-45)

2.33 - Sky Blue Satin Glass #8105. 9" Rolled Edge Bowl. (30-45)

2.34 - Jasper Console Set: #76. 9" Candlesticks and #8105. 10" Rolled Edge Bowl with Black base. (165-195, set)

2.35 - Canary Satin Glass #8105. 12 1/2" Centerpiece Bowl with 'White Daisies' fired enamel decoration. (65-85)

2.36 - Reflex Green #8177. 12" footed Centerpiece Bowl with gold encrusted decoration. (65-85)

2.37 - Crystal #9705. 7" Compote with Minton Gold etched band. (65-80)

2.39 - Amberina Satin Glass 4-3/4" Compote, unknown Line Number. (30-45)

2.38 - Unknown Line Number: left, Black Satin Glass 10" Crimped Bowl on separate base; right, "3-Lite Candelabrum." (75-95, 100-130 pair)

2.40 - Crystal 9 1/2" Compote with 'Canadian Star' Cutting, unknown Line Number. (50-75)

2.41 - Unusual 7-3/4" Compote with Blue bowl and foot joined by Canary/Amber two part stem, attributed to Tiffin. (200-250)

2.42 - 9 1/2" Blue and Canary Compote, attributed to Tiffin. (175-250)

2.43 - Blue and Canary 10" Salver, attributed to Tiffin. (150-200)

Chapter Three
BOXES AND JARS

3.1 - The Sales and Marketing Office of Factory R frequently featured candy boxes and other confectionery novelties in their national advertising campaigns. The #8132. 6" Heart Bon Bon (3.8) appeared in *Crockery and Glass Journal*, October 28, 1926, p. 14.

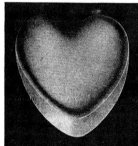
3.2 - #012. 8 1/2" Rose Pink Candy Jar. (45-60)

3.3 - #179. 7 1/2" Conic Candy Box in Canary, Black, and Emerald Green Satin Glass.
(35-55, 45-65, 40-55)

3.4 - #179. 10" Candy Box in Sky Blue, Amberina, and Emerald Green Satin Glass. (45-55, 55-65, 40-60)

3.5 - #15179. 9 1/2" Candy Box in Black and Canary Satin Glass. (40-60, 35-55)

3.6 - #319. 8" Oval Candy Box in Black and Sky Blue Satin Glass. (50-65 each)

3.7 - #330. 8" Cone Candy Jar in Reflex Green Satin Glass and #9313. 6 1/2" Dancing Girl Puff Box in undecorated Reflex Green Satin. (45-55, 145-165)

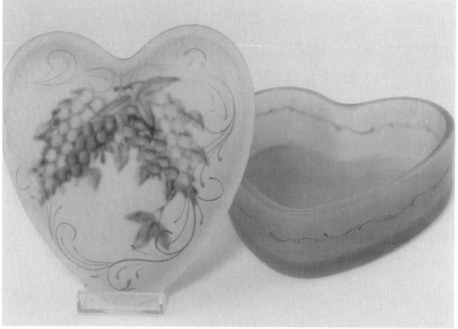

3.8 - Rose Pink Satin Glass #8132. 6" Heart Bon Bon with enameled Grape decoration on inner surface of "crowned" cover. Gold tracery scrolling adorns the surface of the vertical sides of the box as well as the top of the domed cover. (95-115)

3.9 - Black Satin Glass #8142. 6" Bon Bon or Powder Box with Coralene encrusted enamel floral decoration. (145-175)

3.10 - Black Satin Glass #8142. 6" Bon Bon or Powder Box with Coralene encrusted multi-colored floral enamel decoration and Minnesota-based decorating firm's original "Peacock Products" label on bottom. (145-175)

3.12 - Black Satin Glass #8142. 6" Bon Bon or Powder Box with Coralene encrusted enamel floral decoration. (145-175)

3.11 - "McCourt Studios, Minneapolis" label on #8142. 6" Black Satin Glass Bon Bon or Powder Box. The #8142. "embossed floral design" base was originally advertised as a "Squat Bowl" but, with the addition of a matching cover, was adaptable to many uses. It is usually advertised as a Bon Bon or Powder Box today.

3.13 - Detail of pink enameled floral embossment with Coralene encrustation.

3.14 - Canary Satin Glass: left, #8308. 6" Bon Bon or
Powder Box; right, #151. 6 1/2"
Cupped Flower Bowl. (30-50, 20-35)

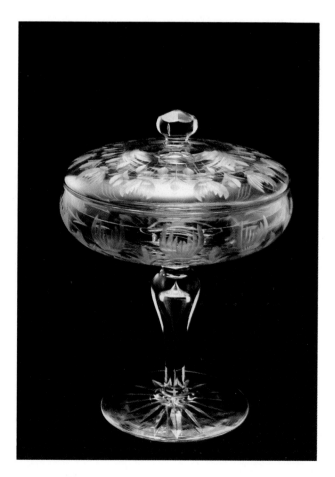

3.15 - Doris Cutting on Crystal #9556. 6" Bon Bon
with inverted teardrop stem.
(65-85)

3.16 - #9557. 1/2-lb. Candy Jar, Blue with Canary trim.
(90-125)

3.17 - Crystal #9557. 1/2-lb. Candy Jar with Amber trim and Julia Etching. (95-135)

3.18 - Crystal #9557. 1/2-lb. Candy Jar with Green trim and Bluebell Cutting, a.k.a. Columbine. (95-135)

3.19 - Detail of Bluebell/Columbine Cutting on #9557. Candy Jar (3.18).

3.20 - Sky Blue Satin Glass #16256. 5" Bath Salt Jar with cover. (85-115)

NEW OVAL CANDY BOX

THE new 15319 Oval Candy Box is quite an innovation. It is 8½ inches long by 5¼ inches wide, and is available in black, blue, green and canary, bright or satin finish.

It can be had with four partitions, retailing for $1.75 to $2, or plain inside, retailing at about $1.25 to $1.50, as desired. A fine item for Fall selling that should be remembered on your next order.

UNITED STATES GLASS COMPANY
PITTSBURGH, PENNSYLVANIA
OFFICES IN ALL PRINCIPAL CITIES

Visit Our New Display and Sales Rooms—Pottery & Glass Bldg., 954 Liberty Ave., Pittsburgh, Pa.

3.22 -*Crockery and Glass Journal*, October 1, 1925, p. 25. The #319. 8" Oval Candy Box was available with four partitions or "plain inside." (3.6)

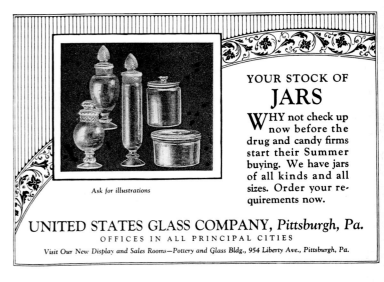

YOUR STOCK OF
JARS

WHY not check up now before the drug and candy firms start their Summer buying. We have jars of all kinds and all sizes. Order your requirements now.

Ask for illustrations

UNITED STATES GLASS COMPANY, *Pittsburgh, Pa.*
OFFICES IN ALL PRINCIPAL CITIES
Visit Our New Display and Sales Rooms—Pottery and Glass Bldg., 954 Liberty Ave., Pittsburgh, Pa.

3.21 - Reflex Green Satin Glass #16256. 5" Bath Salt Jar with cover. (85-115)

3.23 - *Crockery and Glass Journal*, March 13, 1924, p.7. Apothecary Jars, Candy Displays, and Food Preserver Boxes were always good sellers in retail and wholesale outlets.

Chapter Four
CANDLEHOLDERS

4.1 - Satin Glass #10. Low Candleholders: rear, Amber, Black, Emerald Green, and Crystal; front, Reflex Green, Canary, and Sky Blue. (all colors, 20-30 pair)

Candleholders are priced 'per pair' unless otherwise stated.

4.2 - Black Satin Glass #10. Low Candleholders and #15319. 10" Flared Compote, all with unknown gold stencil decoration. (85-125 set)

4.6 - #319. Handled Candleholders: Amberina, Canary, and Black Satin Glass. (65-85 pair)

4.3 - #13. Low Candleholder in Old Gold. (20-25 pair)

4.7 - #97. 'Poppy' Low Candleholders in undecorated Rose Pink Satin Glass. (60-85)

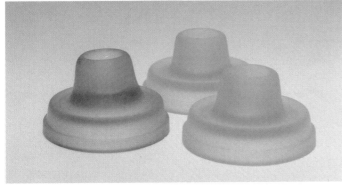

4.4 - #13. Low Candleholders in Sky Blue and Canary Satin Glass. (30-45 pair)

4.5 - Reflex Green Satin Glass: left, #310. Low Candleholders; right, domed #97. Low Candleholders. (30-45 pair)

4.8 - #97. 'Poppy' Low Candleholders in Black Satin Glass with Coralene encrusted enamel decoration. (100-125)

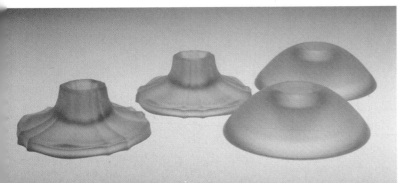

4.9 - #66. 7 1/2" Royal Blue
Candleholders. (75-100)

4.10 - #66. 7 1/2" Amethyst
Candleholders. (65-85)

4.11 - #66. 7 1/2" Emerald Green
Candleholders. (55-75)

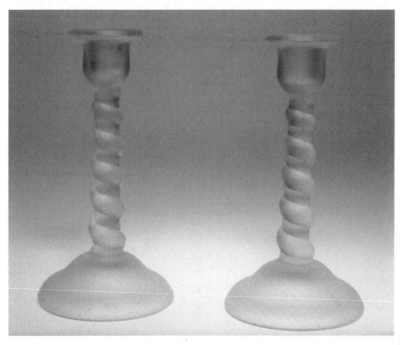

4.12 - #66. 7 1/2" Canary Satin Glass Candleholders. (50-70)

4.14 - Amberina Satin Glass #66. 7 1/2" Candleholders. (65-85)

4.13 - Reflex Green Satin Glass: #66. 7 1/2" Candleholders with #315. 7 1/2" Compote. (65-85, 45-60)

4.15 - Amberina #75. 9 1/2"
Candleholder. (65-85)

4.16 - Amethyst Satin Glass #76.
8" Candleholder. (65-85)

4.17 - Sky Blue #76. 9"
Candleholder. (110-125)

4.18 - Emerald Green Satin Glass: #76. 9"
Candleholders and #15179. Cupped Bowl on Black
Satin Glass base. (65-85 pair, 45-60)

4.19 - Royal Blue Satin Glass Console Set: #76. 8"
Gold Line Decoration No. 1 Candlesticks and #15179.
10" Handled Bowl. The accompanying Royal Blue "hot
weather candles", a 1924 production item at Factory
R in Tiffin, Ohio, were made of glass and add to the
rarity of this 'set.' (400-500 set)

4.21 - Amber Satin Glass #79. 6" Candleholder. (45-
65)

4.20 - Canary Satin Glass #78. 11 1/2" Sconce, scarce
in any color. (175-250)

4.22 - #80. 8" Candleholders, Crystal with Ruby Stain.
(75-95)

4.23 - Reflex Green Satin Glass #81. 7" Candleholders. (40-60)

4.24 - Black Satin Glass Console Set: #82. 8 1/2" Candleholders and #15179. 8 1/2" Flower Bowl with unknown Silver Overlay decoration. (450-550)

4.25 - Sky Blue Satin Glass #82. 8 1/2" Candleholders. (50-75)

4.26 - Black Satin Glass Console Set: #84. 10" Candleholders and #179. 9" Low Foot Compote with unknown Silver Overlay decoration. (250-350)

4.27 - #84. 10" Candleholders, unknown opaque color name. (85-125)

4.29 - #151. 9" Candleholders, orange painted Crystal blank with Silver Overlay 'Peacock' decoration. (55-75)

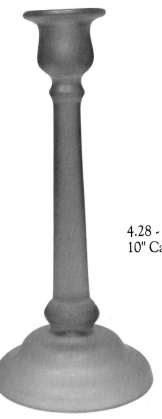

4.28 - Sky Blue Satin Glass #84. 10" Candleholder. (55-70)

4.30 - Detail of Silver Overlay 'Peacock' decoration (4.29).

4.31 - Amber #310. Console Set: 9" Candleholders and 11 1/2" Open Work Compote. (85-105)

4.33 - Green Stretch Glass #310. 9" Candleholders. Research continues regarding correct terminology. (100-145)

4.32 - Amberina Satin Glass #310. 9" Candleholders. (65-95)

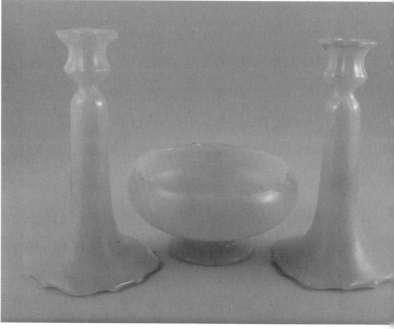

4.34 - Yellow Stretch Glass #310. 9" Candleholders and matching 7 1/2" Cupped Bowl, unknown Line Number. Research continues. (65-95, 35-55)

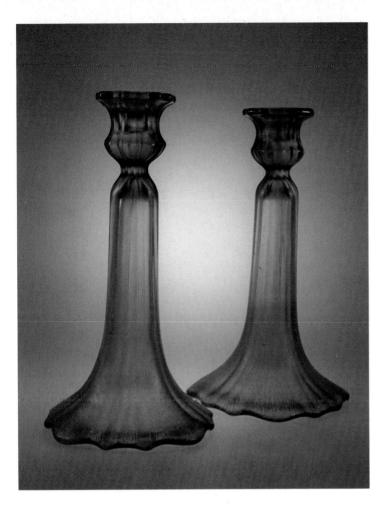

4.35 - Sky Blue Stretch Glass #15310. 9" Candleholders. (60-85)

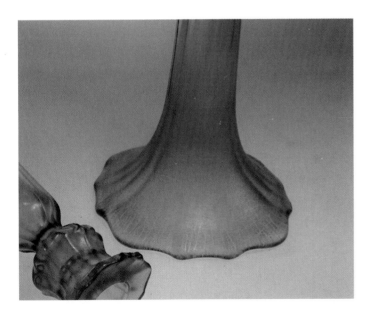

4.36 - Detail of Stretch Glass 'texture.' (4.35)

4.37 - Canary Satin Glass Candleholders: left #66. 7 1/2"; center #315. 9"; right #315. 9 3/4". (50-70, 50-70, 60-80)

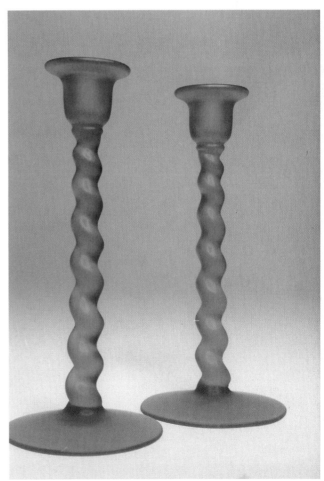

4.38 - Sky Blue Satin Glass #315. 9" Candleholders. (65-85)

47

4.39 - Amberina Satin Glass #315. Console Set: 9 3/4" Candleholders with 7 1/2" High Foot Compote. (100-150, 65-75)

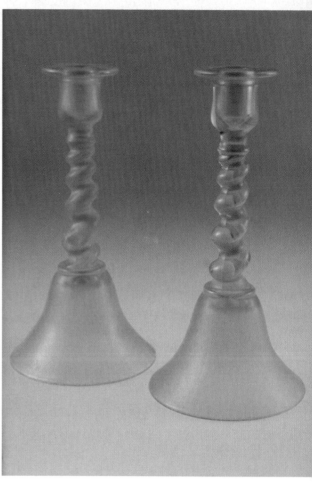

4.41 - Canary Stretch Glass #315. 9-3/4" Candleholders. (100-150)

4.40 - Crystal Stretch Glass #315. 9-3/4" Candleholders. (85-125)

4.42 - Sky Blue Satin Glass #315. Console Set: 9-3/4" Candleholders with 10" Low Foot Compote. (75-95, 45-65)

4.45 - Amberina Satin Glass #15319. 8" Candleholders and matching #15179. 8 1/2" Cupped Rim Flower Bowl, both with Silver Overlay decoration. (350-425 set)

4.43 - Black Satin Glass #15319. 8" Candleholders with enamel and gold trim. (75-95)

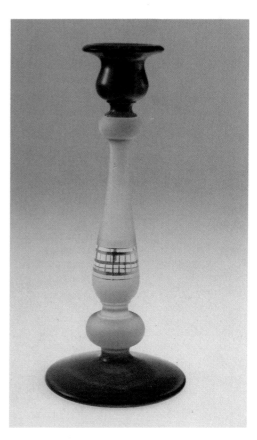

4.44 - Sky Blue Satin Glass #319. 8" Candleholders with enamel and gold trim. (80-100)

4.46 - Crystal #319. 10" Candleholder with Ruby Stain base and candle block. The combination of satinization with the gold decorated bright panel is considered unusual. (50-60 single)

4.47 - Black Satin Glass #319. 10" Candleholders with gold trim. (75-115)

4.48 - Black Satin Glass #15320. 10" Candleholders, enameled 'Parrot' decoration. (85-115)

4.49 - Black Satin Glass 6-3/8" Triple Branch Cande-labrum, unknown Line Number. (100-150 pair)

4.50 - Crystal #15309 "Betsy Ross" 14. 8" Candleholders. (65-95)

4.51 - Canary with Blue trim: #9705. 7" Compote with 9 1/2" Candleholders, unknown Line Number. (100-150, 200-250)

4.52 - Crystal #14194. 8" Candleholder with unlisted floral cutting. (225-275)

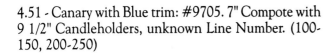

4.53 - Detail of floral cutting on #14194. 8" Candleholder (4.52).

4.54 - Reflex Green #8153. 12" Centerpiece Bowl and
Emerald Green 7" Candleholders with Crystal trim,
Line Number unknown. (85-115, 100-135 pair)

*The United States Glass Co., Pittsburgh, Pa., with New York
showrooms at 1107 Broadway present their No. 8177 centerpiece set in green and pink glass either plain or with gold
border encrustation. The graceful lines of the shape are particularly appealing.*

4.55 - The #8177. Centerpiece Bowl (2.36) and Low
Candleholders were introduced in 1929 (*Crockery and
Glass Journal*).

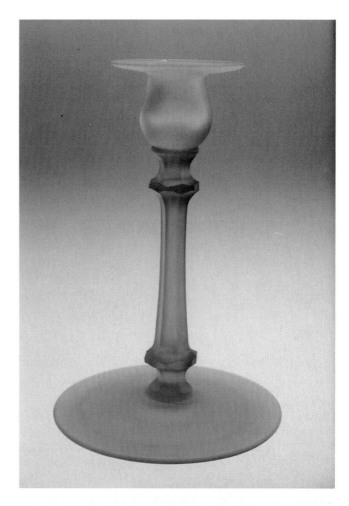

4.56 - Emerald Green Satin Glass
7" Candleholder with Crystal
trim, unknown Line Number.
(110-140)

4.57 - 9 1/2" Candleholder, orange painted Crystal blank. Unknown Line Number. (30-40)

4.58 - Canary Satin Glass 9" Candlesticks attributed to Factory R. (45-65)

4.59 - In 1927, to harmonize with the #8127. 13 1/2" Bulb Box, "Mythological" panels were added to the #18. Low Candleholder (7.52) (Crockery and Glass Journal, January 13, 1927, p. 34).

Chapter Five
DECORATIONS AND TEXTURES

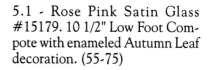

AUTUMN LEAF Decoration

5.1 - Rose Pink Satin Glass #15179. 10 1/2" Low Foot Compote with enameled Autumn Leaf decoration. (55-75)

5.2 - Rose Pink Satin Glass #151. 8" Cupped Dahlia Vase with enameled Autumn Leaf decoration. (65-85)

5.3 - Brilliancy Line #15328. 8 1/2" Console Bowls in Amber and Reflex Green. (35-65 each)

5.4 - Brilliancy Line #15328. Console Set in Canary: 8" Candleholders and 8 1/2" Bowl. (55-75 pair, 35-50)

5.5 - Brilliancy Line #15328. 8" Candleholders and 7 1/2" Cupped Rose Bowl in Reflex Green. (55-75, 50-70)

5.6 - Brilliancy Line #15328. 7 1/2" Cupped Rose Bowl
in Sky Blue. (85-100)

5.7 - Brilliancy Line #15328. 8" Candleholders in Sky
Blue. (90-110)

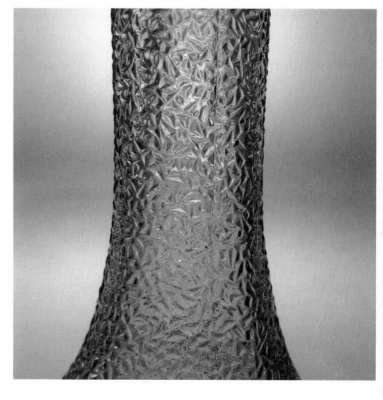

5.8 - Detail of textured Brilliancy Line (5.7).

5.9 - Brilliancy Line #179. 7 1/2" Conic Candy Jar and cover in Canary. (55-70)

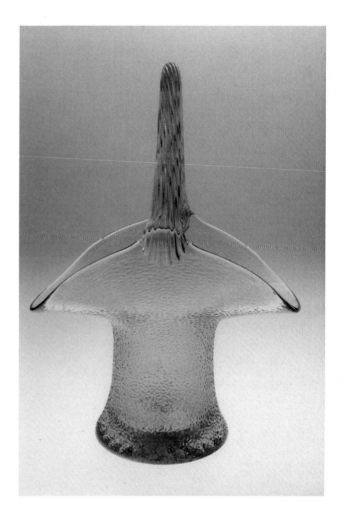

5.10 - Brilliancy Line #15328. 10-3/4" "No. 1 Basket" in Sky Blue. (95-125)

5.11 - Brilliancy Line #15328.: left, 12" Amber "No. 2 Basket"; right, 6" Sky Blue Vase. (70-95, 45-65)

CRAQUELLE Ware

5.12 - Craquelle #194. 9 1/2" Jug in Crystal with Green trim. (150-200)

5.13 - Craquelle #117. 9 1/2" covered Jug in Blue with Canary trim. (225-275)

5.14 - Craquelle #117. 7 1/2" open Jug in Canary with Blue trim. (175-225)

ECHEC Decoration

ECHEC Decoration is a combination of 'bright and satin blocks' on black glass with gold edge.

Echec's Pattern on Comport

Echec's Pattern 16261 Flower Holder.

(PAT. APPL. FOR)

New Echec's Glassware—
A Fine Holiday Line

IN THIS decoration we have achieved the unusual by combining both satin and brilliant finish in a bold square pattern edged with gold bands. The items illustrated are typical of the line, which is wide and includes pieces that are particularly suitable for the Holiday trade and many others that will find use in practically every room in the home.

Write for illustrations and prices on the complete line.

UNITED STATES GLASS COMPANY
PITTSBURGH, PENNA.

SALES OFFICES IN ALL LARGE CITIES

"Visit Our Permanent Exhibit at 954 Liberty Avenue when in Pittsburgh"

5.15 - *Crockery and Glass Journal*, December 3, 1925, p. 27.

5.16 - ECHEC #8098. 7 1/2" footed Rose Bowl on undecorated base. (95-130)

5.17 - ECHEC #15179. 8" Cupped Compote. (100-125)

ICED Decoration

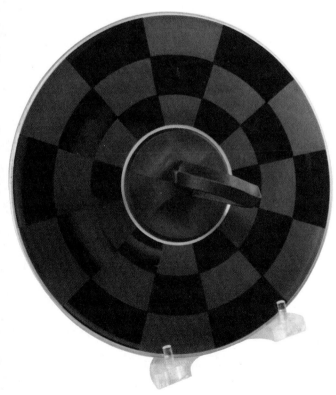

5.18 - ECHEC #15151. 8" Cupped Dahlia Vase (also made 10 1/2"). (100-150)

5.20 - All-Crystal ICED Decoration #0275. 10-3/4" covered Jug. The ICED Line was also produced in Crystal with Amber, Blue, Green, or Canary trim. (125-175)

5.19 - ECHEC Decoration: left, #15320. 10" Center Handled Cake Plate; right, #320. Cheese Plateau on 10" Cracker Plate with center indent. (95-115, 100-125)

JACK FROST
Decoration

5.21 - JACK FROST Line in Emerald Green: left, #8076. 11" Open Work Orange Bowl; right, #315. 7 1/2" Low Foot Compote. (55-85, 50-75)

5.22 - JACK FROST Line #18. 4" Candleholders in Rose Pink. (40-65)

5.23 - JACK FROST Line in Canary: #84. 10" Candleholders and #315. 7 1/2" High Foot Compote. (100-125, 65-85)

5.24 - JACK FROST Line #9574. 6" Basket in Rose Pink. (100-150)

5.25 - JACK FROST Line: left, Crystal #9574. 6" Basket; right, Canary #315. 10" Low Foot Compote. (75-105, 665-95)

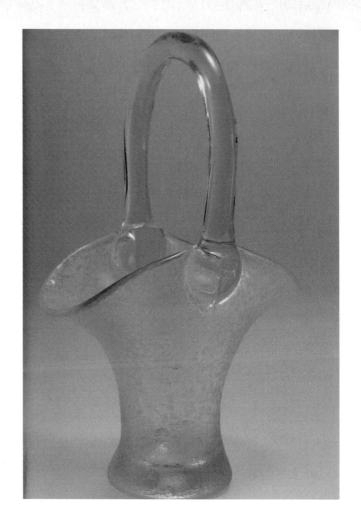

5.26 - JACK FROST Line #444. 12-oz. handled Lemonade, Crystal with Green trim. (30-40)

KIMBERLY Decoration

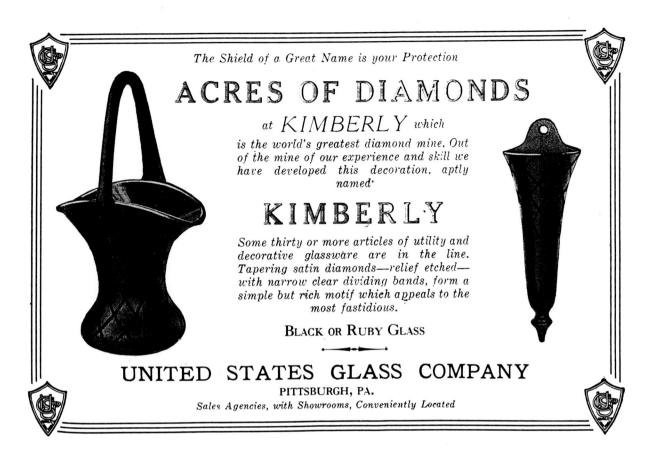

5.27 - *Crockery and Glass Journal,* June 17, 1926, p. 31.

5.28 - KIMBERLY Decoration on Ruby #8098. 7 1/2" covered Rose Bowl with Ruby Satin Glass base. Considered rare due to 'decoration' on this color. (275-375)

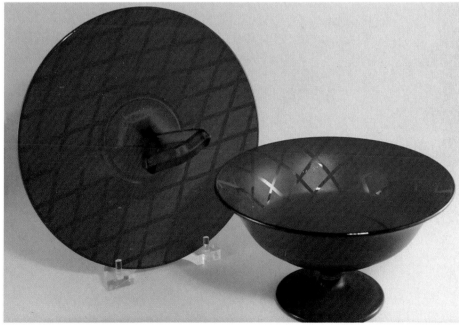

5.29 - KIMBERLY Decoration on Ruby: left, #179. 10" handled Cake Plate; right, #330. 8 1/2" footed Bowl. (150-200, 175-225)

5.30 - KIMBERLY Decoration on Black: left, #320. 9" Wall Vase; right, #320. 9" Console Bowl. (115-130, 65-85)

5.31 - KIMBERLY Decoration on Ruby: left, #330. 8 1/2" Low Foot Compote; right, #320. 10" Candlesticks. (150-200, 250-300)

5.32 - KIMBERLY Decoration on Ruby: left, #330. 5 1/2" Compote; right, #320. 8 1/2" Console Bowl. (150-200, 125-175)

5.33 - KIMBERLY Decoration on Ruby: left, #9723. 10" Bud Vase; right, #330. 5" Low Foot Bon Bon, no cover. (125-175, 85-110)

64

MEFFORD Decoration

MEFFORD Decoration is a gold 'Block Band' design on Black Satin Glass.

5.34 - The MEFFORD Line #179. 9 1/2" Flared Console Bowl was paired with different bases and candleholders to provide a wide choice of Console Sets for the American homemaker.

5.35 - MEFFORD Decoration: #179. 9 1/2" Flared Console Bowl with base and #319. 10" Candleholders. (55-75, 75-95)

5.36 - MEFFORD Decoration: #319. 12" Rolled Edge Fruit Bowl with base and #66. 7 1/2" Candleholders. (65-85, 80-100)

5.37 - MEFFORD Line #151. 8" Cupped Dahlia Vases. (60-85 each)

5.38 - MEFFORD Line: left, #151. 10 1/2" Flared Dahlia Vase; center, #151. 10" Plate; right, #15319. 7 1/2" High Foot Compote. (55-75, 35-55, 60-90)

5.39 - MEFFORD Line: #15179. 4 1/2" Sweet Pea Bowl with gold decorated base and #10. 3-3/4" Candleholders. (75-95, 30-50)

PURITAN and Other Enamels

5.40 - ENAMEL Decorations on Bright Finish ware: left, PURITAN Decoration on #15179. 10 1/2" Low Bowl with painted black base; center, COSMO variant decoration on #179. 7 1/2" High Foot Compote with painted black base; right, #15179. 8" Urn Vase with painted beige base and unknown enamel decoration. (85-110, 55-75, 65-85)

5.41 - Rose Pink Satin #151. 4" Whipped Cream with unknown bird and floral enamel decoration. (65-85)

5.42 - Left, Crystal Satin Glass #179. 10" Center Handled Cake Plate with enamel decoration applied to the under surface; right, Crystal Stretch Glass #310. 6 1/2" Compote. (70-90, 75-95)

RAJAH Decoration

#22030. RAJAH Line, one of Tiffin's most elusive decorations, is a 'gold rubber stamp design' on Black Satin blanks.

5.43 - Left, RAJAH Decoration on Black Satin Glass #16261. 8 1/2" Open Work Vase. (95-115)

5.44 - Detail of #22030 RAJAH "gold rubber stamp design" (5.43).

SATIN RIBBON Decoration

SATIN RIBBON Decoration is a combination of 'bright and satin stripes' on Bright Black blanks.

5.45 - SATIN RIBBON Decoration on #319. 8 1/2"
Oval Candy Box. (165-225)

5.46 - SATIN RIBBON Decoration on #151. 8"
Cupped Dahlia Vase. (100-125)

5.47 - SATIN RIBBON Decoration on #16261.
8 1/2" Open Work Vase. (90-115)

Stippled Ice Tea Set

A low priced ice tea set in the new stippled glass effect. Order by No. 6461, 4 pint jug and 12 oz. Fancy Shape Ice Tea, Stippled. Packs 12 sets per barrel. Also supplied No. 6450 straight shape jug and ice teas at same prices.

UNITED STATES GLASS COMPANY
PITTSBURGH, PENNSYLVANIA
OFFICES IN ALL PRINCIPAL CITIES

Visit Our New Display and Sales Rooms—Pottery & Glass Bldg., 954 Liberty Ave., Pittsburgh, Pa.

5.48 -*Crockery and Glass Journal*, July 31, 1924, p. 7. "Stippled Glassware" is one of the earliest textured lines produced by Tiffin and not easy to find.

5.49 - "Stippled" #6461. 9" Jug, Amber with Jasper trim. (150-200)

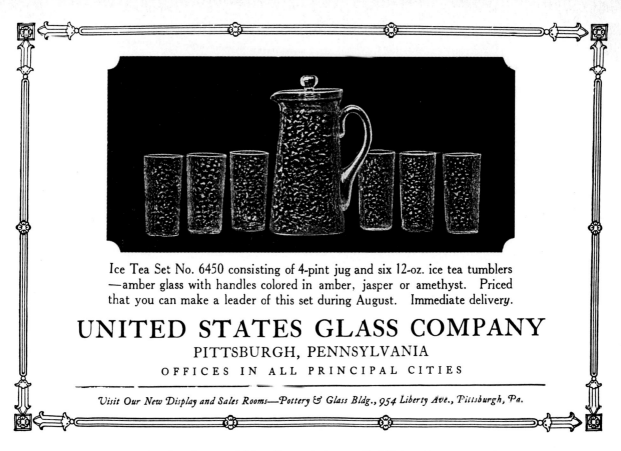

Ice Tea Set No. 6450 consisting of 4-pint jug and six 12-oz. ice tea tumblers —amber glass with handles colored in amber, jasper or amethyst. Priced that you can make a leader of this set during August. Immediate delivery.

UNITED STATES GLASS COMPANY
PITTSBURGH, PENNSYLVANIA
OFFICES IN ALL PRINCIPAL CITIES

Visit Our New Display and Sales Rooms—Pottery & Glass Bldg., 954 Liberty Ave., Pittsburgh, Pa.

5.50 -*Crockery and Glass Journal*, August 7, 1924, p. 7.

Stippled Glassware
At Popular Prices and With a Fall Appeal.

Made in Blue, Green, Amber and Canary.

No. 15328 Stippled Conic Candy Jar and Cover. Will retail at about $1.00.

No. 15328 Stippled 10" Cheese and Cracker. Will retail at about $1.50.

No. 15328 Stippled Handled Cake Plate. Will retail at about $1.00.

Also an 8-inch Salad Plate to Retail at about $6 to $7 a dozen.

UNITED STATES GLASS COMPANY
PITTSBURGH, PENNSYLVANIA
OFFICES IN ALL PRINCIPAL CITIES

Visit Our New Display and Sales Rooms—Pottery & Glass Bldg., 954 Liberty Ave., Pittsburgh, Pa.

5.51 -*Crockery and Glass Journal*, August 13, 1925, p. 7.

Other decorations, textures, and optics are
shown in the following trade journal advertisements, *courtesy of Jones S.R.S. Archives.*

Meet the
PARAKEET TWINS

THE little glass shakers that were commented upon by
so many visitors at the Glass Exhibit have been im-
proved.

They now are available carrying the likeness in colors of
the Parakeet twins—"Salty and Peppy," hand painted in
yellow, red, green and black. They are available in light
green, light blue, canary and white satin glass and look very
pretty on a white linen tablecloth.

Order by No. 6207.

UNITED STATES GLASS COMPANY
PITTSBURGH, PENNSYLVANIA
OFFICES IN ALL PRINCIPAL CITIES

Visit Our New Display and Sales Rooms—Pottery & Glass Bldg., 954 Liberty Ave., Pittsburgh, Pa.

5.52 - #6207. Shaker Set with unfired enamel "PARA-
KEET TWINS" decoration. (*Crockery and Glass Journal,* May 7, 1926, p. 8)

5.53 - Unfired enamel "#14 PARROT" decoration.
(*Crockery and Glass Journal,* April 29, 1926, p. 22)

PARROT DECORATION No. 14
ON
LIGHT GREEN SATIN GLASS

INTRODUCED at the Pittsburgh Show during
January, this unique conception has proven one of
the most popular lines put out in recent years.

The gay little parrot, in colors, perched on a twig,
is the principal motif, and the decoration is com-
pleted and balanced by solid black lines around the
base and top of each piece.

Illustrated are No. 320 Wall Vase, No. 330 Conic
Candy Jar and No. 330 Candleholder, and the line
consists of twenty useful Boudoir and Decorative
pieces, all of which are surprisingly low in price, af-
fording the dealer handsome profits.

This Line is a Leader for Gift Shops

UNITED STATES GLASS CO.,
PITTSBURGH, PA.

*Our Sales Representatives, in All Principal Cities, have samples, or we will
forward color sheet and prices on request.*

72

The New Dana Decoration

A decoration of rare beauty consisting of a floral design in gold over a broad band of stippled blue.

Comports, plates, candlesticks, cheese and cracker sets, whipped cream sets, plates, handled cake and many other useful and attractive pieces.

UNITED STATES GLASS COMPANY

General Offices and Salesrooms

South Ninth and Bingham Sts., Pittsburgh, Pa.

5.54 - Fired enamel and gold "DANA" decoration.
(*Crockery and Glass Journal*, February 1, 1923, p. 8)

The New Glendale

Showing two of the many beautiful and useful pieces finished in the new Glendale decoration.

A dainty design of pink rose buds and a stippled band of green edged with gold.

UNITED STATES GLASS COMPANY

General Offices and Salesrooms

South Ninth and Bingham Sts., Pittsburgh, Pa.

5.55 - Fired enamel and gold "GLENDALE" decoration. (*Crockery and Glass Journal*, February 8, 1923, p. 8)

5.56 - Fired enamel and gold "CONNEAUT" decoration. (*Crockery and Glass Journal*, February 15, 1923, p. 15)

5.57 - Fired enamel "POPPY" decoration. (*Crockery and Glass Journal*, October 7, 1926, p. 18)

5.58 - Fired enamel "FORGET-ME-NOT" decoration. (*Crockery and Glass Journal,* November 25, 1926, p. 18)

5.59 - "LUSTERLINE" or "LUSTRE LINE," research continues on this line of TIFFINware. (*Crockery and Glass Journal,* March 8, 1923, p. 44)

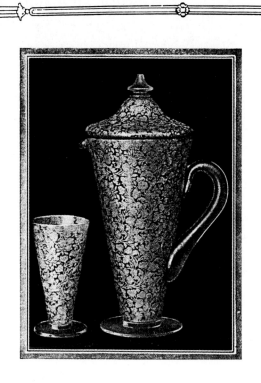
5.60 - In the Twenties, Tiffin produced a number of 'all-over' etchings, including the "TAPESTRY" Etching which was named by Mrs. Weatherman. (*Crockery and Glass Journal*, March 5, 1925, p. 54)

5.61 - This is the only advertisement for TIFFIN "SATIN GLASS" in the Jones S.R.S. Archives. (*Crockery and Glass Journal*, January 11, 1923, p. 9)

"EBON-GOLD-BLOCK"
DECORATION

A dignified decoration, consisting of alternate mat and burnished coin-gold blocks, in a band about ⅝ in. wide, on lustrous black satined blanks. This line appeals strongly to the buyer who wants the best in fancy glassware.

Bon Bons; Candy and Cigarette Boxes; Console and Centerpiece Bowls; Low Candleholders and High Candlesticks; Low and High-foot Comports; Vases; Dresser Sets; etc., etc. Color Plate 285 shows the line.

NO. 320—7 in.
HIGH-FOOT
COMPORT

UNITED STATES GLASS COMPANY
PITTSBURGH, PA.
Sales Offices in Seventeen Principal Cities

5.62 - "EBON-GOLD-BLOCK" Line is an elusive collectible on the current market. (*Crockery and Glass Journal,* January 27, 1927, p. 21)

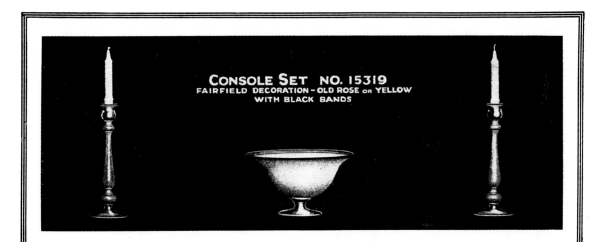

CONSOLE SET NO. 15319
FAIRFIELD DECORATION - OLD ROSE or YELLOW
WITH BLACK BANDS

UNITED STATES GLASS COMPANY
General Offices and Salesrooms
South Ninth and Bingham Sts., Pittsburgh, Pa.

New York: 1107 Broadway
E. T. W. Craig. Representative
Philadelphia: 10th and Market Sts.
J. A. Hemple, Representative
San Francisco: 682 Mission Street
F. M. Dunn, Representative

Boston: 99 Bedford Street
M. A. Lovell. Representative
Los Angeles, 643 South Olive Street
J. F Stirk. Representative
Dallas: Southland Hotel Building
D. D. Otstott. Inc.. Representative

Baltimore: 110 Hopkins Place
John A. Dobson Co., Representative
Chicago: 30 East Randolph Street
F. T. Renshaw, Representative
St. Louis: 1017 Olive St.
J. Donald Fisher, Representative

Denver: 404 Jacobson Building Norton C. Boyer. Representative

5.63 - "FAIRFIELD" decoration. The reader will note that Tiffin's *Rose Pink* was called *OLD ROSE* in 1923. (*Crockery and Glass Journal,* January 25, 1923, p. 12)

ARTISTIC 15331 PIECES

Pictured above are cheese and cracker set, lily vase, high foot comport, dahlia vase, fruit bowl and salad plate. These are typical of the spiral optic 15331 line, available in green, amber and canary. Write for illustrations and prices.

UNITED STATES GLASS COMPANY
PITTSBURGH, PENNSYLVANIA
OFFICES IN ALL PRINCIPAL CITIES

Visit Our New Display and Sales Rooms—Pottery & Glass Bldg., 954 Liberty Ave., Pittsburgh, Pa.

5.64 - Tiffin "SPIRAL OPTIC."(*Crockery and Glass Journal*, October 22, 1925, p. 27)

UNITED STATES GLASS COMPANY
PITTSBURGH, PA.

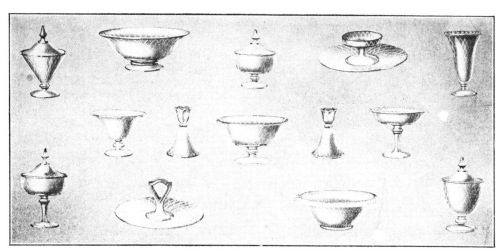

NO. 333 DIAMOND OPTIC PATTERN
GREEN, AMBER AND MULBERRY

AN ATTRACTIVE LINE of Tableware, in the wanted colors, at prices which draw trade and make a quick turn-over. See samples and get prices at office of our nearest Sales Representative, or write us for color sheet illustrating principal items.

5.65 - Tiffin "DIAMOND OPTIC" is seen less often than other Tiffin optics. (*Crockery and Glass Journal*, March 25, 1926, p. 25)

5.66 - Tiffin "NARROW OPTIC." (*Crockery and Glass Journal*, October 9, 1924, p. 9)

5.67 - Tiffin "WIDE OPTIC" with gold encrusted border. In 1924, readers will note, the shield crest was identified as a " Banner Gold Label." (*Crockery and Glass Journal*, 1924, p. 7)

Chapter Six
FIGURALS

Cats and dogs, fish and frogs, and other 'Tiffin creatures' of the 1920s and 1930s are highly prized today. The elusive 'lady from Tiffin' introduces a sampling of other collectible Tiffin figurals.

Draped Nude Stem

With factory terminology unavailable, the Tiffin Draped Nude Stem has been aptly named by today's collectors of Tiffin Glass. Although nothing relating to form and figure is left to the imagination, the torso, other than her shoulders, arms and left knee, is, indeed, fully draped. Tiffin's Draped Nude is easily distinguishable from similar items produced by other glass companies during this period since, poised with left knee bent forward, her figural profile is not only distinctive but also provocative. With a comparatively short production run, from the 1930s into the 1950s, Draped Nude Stems are considered rare.

6.1 - The Tiffin draped nude stem itself was produced in Royal Blue, Reflex Green, and Crystal, with both Bright and Satin Finishes. The disc foot and blown bowl are Crystal, and the bowl is usually non-optic. The detail of the Royal Blue example shows the singular protrusion of her left knee. Two bowl shapes are known, the most common closely resembling the bowl of Tiffin's #17603. Stem Line. Bowls similar to the #15040. Stem Line (6.4) are seen less often.

6.2 - TIFFIN DRAPED NUDE Wine, Reflex Green and Crystal. (150-225)

6.3 - Crystal Satin DRAPED NUDE #17603. Line with Crystal bowl and disc foot: Champagne, Water Goblet, Cordial, and Wine. (100-150, 100-150, 125-175, 100-150)

6.4 - Bowl differentials on DRAPED NUDE Stems: left, all-Crystal Water Goblet with #15040. bowl which differs from the more common #17603. bowl at center and right; center, Wine with Reflex Green stem; right, all-Crystal Wine. (125-175, 150-225, 100-150)

6.5 - Royal Blue Satin DRAPED NUDE #17603. Line with Crystal bowl and foot: Champagne, Water Goblet, Wine, and Cordial. (125-175, 125-175, 125-175, 150-200)

6.6 - Black Satin Glass #69. 5 3/4" FROG Candleholders, also made in Bright Finish. (85-100 each)

6.7 - Black Glass #72. 6" FROG Candleholder, produced in both Satin (center) and Bright (left/right) Finish. (85-135, 65-100)

6.8 - Black Satin Glass #78. 7" BULLDOG Doorstop with rhinestone eyes, ranks high on the list of Tiffin rarities. (350-450)

6.9 - #9213. 3 1/2" DOG Ash Tray: left, Black Satin Glass; right, Old Gold Bright Finish. (75-100, 50-75)

6.10 - Canary #8171. 11 1/2" Fish Globe on Black 4 3/4" Dolphin Base. Since both globes and bases are elusive, with the globe commanding the higher price, values are listed individually. (150-200, 100-125)

6.11 - Blue #20122. 11" Fish Globe on Black 4-3/4" Dolphin Base. (200-250, 100-125)

6.12 - Rose Pink DOLPHIN Candleholders, unknown Line Numbers: left, 4 1/2"; right, 8." (90-110, 150-190)

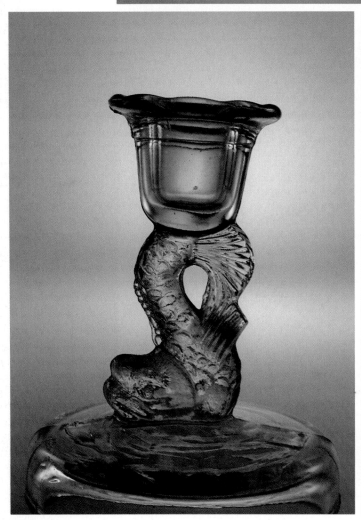

6.13 - Detail of 4 1/2" DOLPHIN Candleholder (6.12).

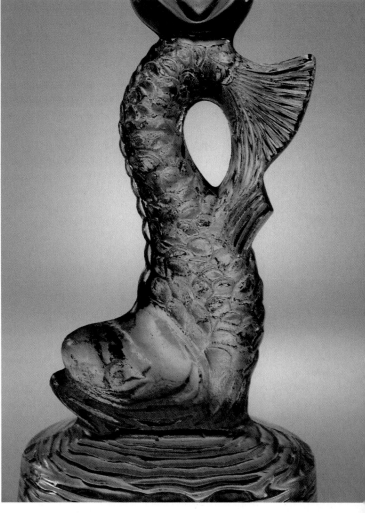

6.14 - Detail of 8" DOLPHIN Candleholder (6.12).

6.15 - Top left and right, Rose Pink 8" DOLPHIN Candleholders; top center, Reflex Green 8" DOLPHIN Candleholder; bottom, Rose Pink 4 1/2" DOLPHIN Candleholder. (150-190, 150-190, 90-110)

6.16 - Reflex Green Satin Glass 4 1/2" DOLPHIN Candleholders. (100-140)

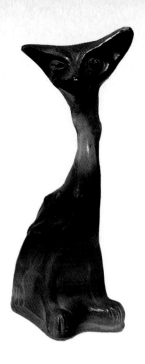

6.17 - This extremely rare 6 1/2" Tiffin feline is catalogued very simply as the "#9445. Cat," with no further descriptive encomiums. He is the sole known example of his breed in captivity since, unlike many other *colored* glass animals in the Tiffin menagerie, the #9445. 6 1/2" Cat was produced as a Crystal blank and then given a brown and beige coat of fired enamel *fur*. (rare)

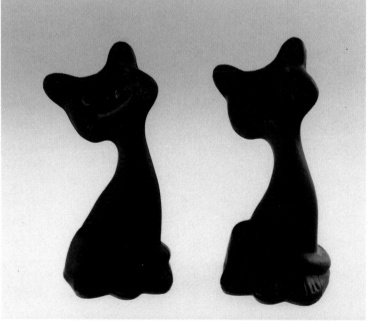

6.18 - The #9446. 6 1/2" GROTESQUE CAT was produced in Bright Black Finish as well as Black Satin Glass and came both decorated and plain. Collectors favor the satin version which is shown on the right. (85-135, 125-175)

6.19 - Black Satin Glass #9446. 6 1/2" GROTESQUE CAT: left, with enamel decoration; right, undecorated. *Decoration* does not increase value for collectors. (125-175 each)

6.20 - Black Satin Glass #9448. 11" LARGE CAT with fired enamel facial highlights. Also available in Bright Finish and/or undecorated, neither of which affects the value. (175-225)

6.21 - Bright Finish #9448. 11" OPAL LARGE CAT, another elusive participant in the parade of Tiffin figurals. (rare)

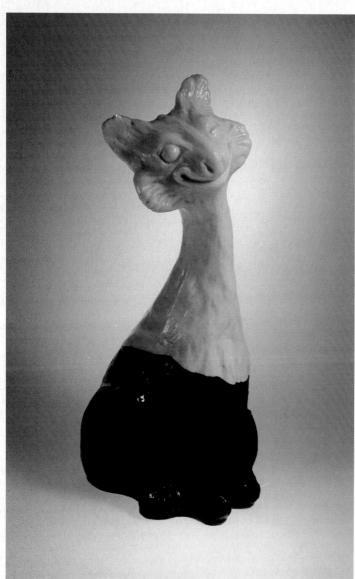

6.22 - This *Bi-Color* version of the #9448. 11" LARGE CAT falls into the 'true Tiffin rarity category,' the only known example of Tiffin *Opal cased Black Glass*. (very rare)

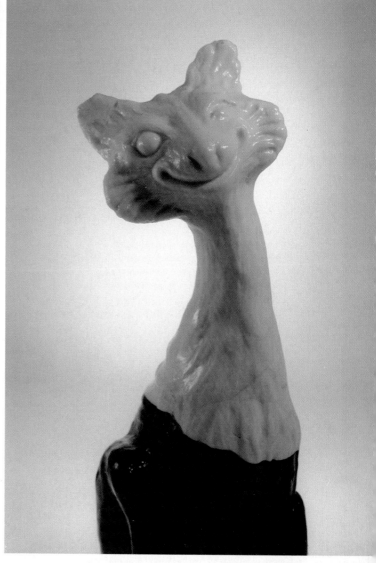

6.23 - Detail of Opal cased Black Glass #9448. 11" LARGE CAT (6.22).

Chapter Seven
FLOWER ARRANGERS AND VASES

Tiffin produced vases for virtually every type of floral arrangement and display. Designs, styles, and shapes were heralded in the fine print of a 1926 trade journal advertisement: "From the daintiest bud, nestling alone, to the largest fully-developed bloom, in masses, there is some suitable receptacle in our varied lines."

Varied, to be sure: "crystal, satin, cut, etched, 'decorated,' gold encrusted, bud, wall, fan, banquet, florist, swung, automobile vases, Red, Royal Blue, Black, Amber, Green, Amethyst, Blue, Canary"— A Vase or Basket for Every Flower!

7.1 - *China, Glass & Lamps,* July 5, 1926.

7.2 - Opal #33. 9-3/4" Vase with *MINTON Gold* decoration. (225-275)

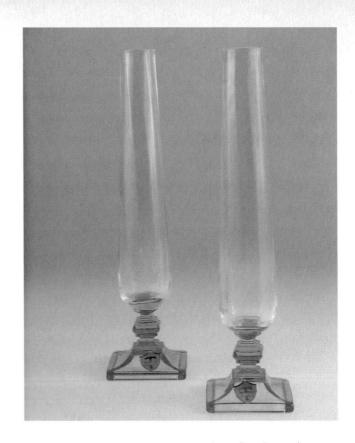

7.4 - Crystal #064. 9 1/2" Vase with Reflex Green base. (55-75 each)

7.3 - Opal #33. 9-3/4" Vase with gold encrusted *CLASSIC Etching*. (275-350)

7.5 - Festoon Optic #064. 5 1/2" Ivy Ball with Reflex Green base. Fry, Cambridge, and Morgantown produced many different styles of 'ivy arrangers,' but this is the only known Tiffin Ivy Ball on record. (100-125)

7.6 - Rose Pink Satin Glass #151. 7" Sweet Pea Vase. (45-65)

7.7 - Left, Sky Blue Satin Glass #151. 9-3/4" Vase with Silver Overlay decoration; center, Reflex Green Satin Glass #151. 6" Vase; right, Sky Blue Satin Glass #179. 9 1/2" Candy Jar with Silver Overlay decoration. (150-200, 35-50, 150-200)

7.8 - #151. Line: left, decorated Crystal Satin Glass 8" Cupped Dahlia Vase; left center, Sky Blue Satin Glass 8 1/2" Lily Vase; right center, Emerald Green Satin Glass 10 1/2" Dahlia Vase; right, decorated Canary Satin Glass 6" Dahlia Vase. (85-110, 45-65, 50-75, 60-90)

7.9 - Black Satin Glass #151. 10 1/2", 8", and 6" Flared Dahlia Vases. (45-65 each)

7.11 - #151. 8" Flared Dahlia Vases in Amberina and Emerald Green Satin Glass. (50-75 each)

7.10 - #151. 6" Flared Dahlia Vases in Black, Sky Blue, and Canary Satin Glass. (45-65 each)

7.12 - Amberina Satin Glass with unknown cutting: left, #151. 10 1/2" Flared Dahlia Vase; right, #320. 9" Low Foot Compote. (100-150 each)

7.13 - Black #151. 6" Flared Dahlia Vase with unusual gold and iridescent enamel decoration. (100-150)

7.14 - Black Satin Glass #151. 8" Flared Dahlia Vase with gold decoration. (115-135)

7.15 - Crystal Satin Glass: left, #151. 8" Flared Dahlia Vase with enamel decoration; right, #16261. 8 1/2" Open Work Flower Arranger Vase. (175-225 each)

7.16 - #151. Black Satin Glass Cupped Dahlia Vases: left, 8" with *MEFFORD* gold decoration; center and right, 10" and 6" undecorated. (60-85, 55-75, 35-50)

7.18 - #151. 8" Black Satin Glass Cupped Dahlia Vase with Ebon-Gold-Block Decoration. (60-80)

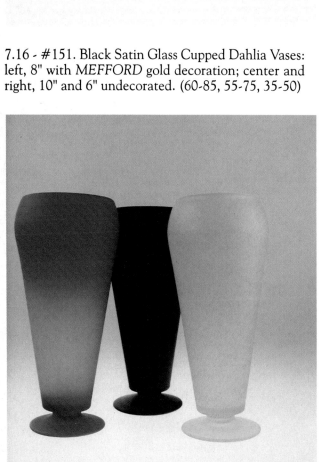

7.17 - #151. 10" Cupped Dahlia Vases in Amberina, Black, and Canary Satin Glass. (55-75, 55-75, 50-70)

7.19 - #151. 8" Black Satin Glass Cupped Dahlia Vase with gold stencil decoration. (75-100)

7.20 - #151. 8" Black Satin Glass Cupped Dahlia Vase with enamel decoration. (100-125)

7.22 - Black Satin Glass #151. 10 1/2" and 6" Cupped Dahlia Vases with Silver Overlay decoration. (350-450, 250-350)

7.21 - Detail of enamel decoration on #151. Black Satin Glass Dahlia Vase (7.20).

7.23 - Black Satin Glass #151. 6" and 10 1/2" Cupped Dahlia Vases with Silver Overlay decoration. (175-225, 300-375)

7.24 - Emerald Green Satin Glass #151. 8" Cupped Dahlia Vase with Silver Overlay decoration. (300-375)

7.26 - #151. Cupped Dahlia Vases: left, 6" Black Satin Glass with enamel and Silver Overlay decoration; center, 6" Sky Blue Satin Glass with Silver Overlay decoration; right, 6" Black Satin Glass with Silver Overlay decoration. (265-295, 185-235, 175-225)

7.25 - Emerald Green Satin Glass #151. 6" Cupped Dahlia Vase with Silver Overlay decoration. (275-350)

7.27 - Detail of Silver Overlay decoration with enamel inset on #151. 6" Black Satin Glass Cupped Dahlia Vase (7.26).

7.28 - #151. 6" Cupped Dahlia Vases: left, Reflex Green Satin Glass with unknown Silver Overlay decoration; right: Emerald Green Satin Glass with *KOBI BASKET* Silver Overlay decoration. (175-225, 200-250)

7.30 - *KOBI BASKET* Silver Overlay decoration on Satin Glass #151. Cupped Dahlia Vases: left, 6" Emerald Green; center, 10" Black; right, 6" Sky Blue. (200-250, 225-275, 175-225)

7.29 - #151. Satin Glass Dahlia Vases: left, Sky Blue 6" Flared with unknown Silver Overlay decoration; right, Emerald Green 8" Cupped with *KOBI BASKET* Silver Overlay decoration. (160-190, 225-275)

7.31 - Detail of *KOBI BASKET* Silver Overlay decoration (7.30).

7.32 - Black Satin Glass #151. 8" Flared and 6" Cupped Dahlia Vases with unknown Silver Overlay decorations. (350-450, 175-225)

7.33 - Detail of Silver Overlay on Black Satin Glass #151. 8" Vase (7.32).

7.34 - Detail of Silver Overlay on Black Satin Glass #151. 6" Vase (7.32).

Tiffin Opaques

Although the illustrated *opaques* are definitely Tiffin shapes, research continues regarding *color names* and *correct Line number* attribution. Reader communication is welcome.

7.35 - #151. *Opaques:* left, 8" Lily Vase; center, 8" Flared Dahlia Vase; right, 8" Cupped Dahlia Vase.

7.37 - *Opaques:* iridized #8076. 10" Open Work Bowl and #151. 6" Flared Dahlia Vase,

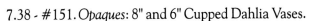

7.38 - #151. *Opaques:* 8" and 6" Cupped Dahlia Vases.

7.36 - #151. *Opaques:* 6" Flared and Cupped Dahlia Vases.

7.39 - #151. *Opaques*: 8" and 6" Cupped Dahlia Vases.

7.42 - #310. 8 1/2" Black Satin Glass Open Work Fan Vase. (45-60)

7.40 - #179. 5" Emerald Green and 7" Canary Satin Glass Urn Vases. (40-50 each)

7.43 - #179. 5" Crystal Urn Vase with enamel decoration and gold trim. (85-115)

7.41 - #179. 5" Blue Urn Vase. (55-75)

7.44 - Detail of enamel decoration (7.43).

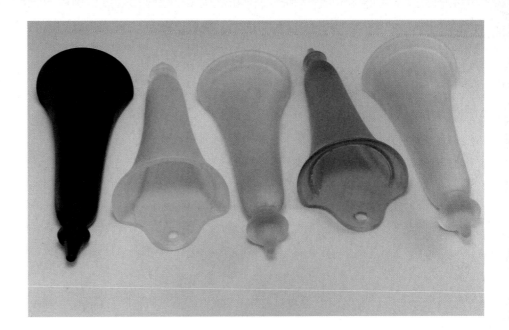

7.45 - #320. 9" Satin Glass Wall Vases: Black, Canary, Rose Pink, Sky Blue, and Reflex Green. (55-75 each)

7.46 - #320. 9" Wall Vases: left, Ruby; center, Royal Blue; right, Ruby Satin Glass with *KIMBERLY Decoration*. (125-175, 100-150, 150-200)

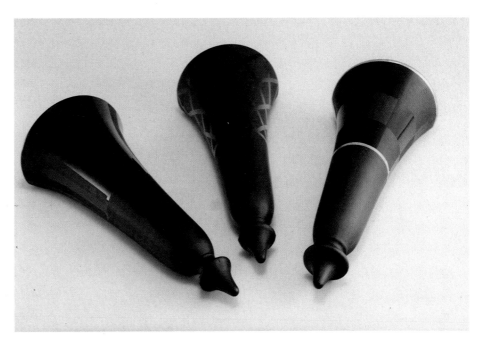

7.47 - #320. 9" Black Wall Vases: left, *RIBBON Decoration* ; center, *KIMBERLY Decoration*; right, *ECHEC Decoration*. (85-105, 110-135, 110-135)

7.48 - Left, #16258. 9" Jasper Wall Vase with wheel cut floral decoration; right, #320. 9" Jasper Satin Glass Wall Vase. (135-165, 115-135)

7.49 - #16258. 9" Satin Glass Wall Vases: top left, Amethyst; bottom left, Canary; top right, Amber; center right, Reflex Green; bottom right, Sky Blue. (75-115 each)

7.50 - #16258. 9" Black Satin Glass Wall Vase with 'Parrot in Flight' Silver Overlay decoration. (150-200)

7.51 - 10" x 10" Satin Glass Wall Vases, unknown Line Number: left, Sky Blue; right, Black. (175-225 each)

7.52 - Reflex Green Satin Glass: left, #8127. 9 1/2" Bulb Box (7.107); right, #18. Low Candleholders. (75-100, 35-55)

7.53 - Amber Satin Glass #8127. 9 1/2" Bulb Box. (70-90)

7.54 - Black Satin Glass: left, #8127. 9 1/2" Bulb Box; right, #18. Low Candleholders. (75-100, 35-55)

7.55 - Rose Pink Satin Glass: left, #8127. 9 1/2" Bulb Box; right, #18. Low Candleholders. (75-100, 35-55)

7.56 - Sky Blue Satin Glass: left, #8127. 9 1/2" Bulb Box; right, #18. Low Candleholders. (75-100, 35-55)

7.57 - Crystal Satin Glass: left, #8127. 9 1/2" Bulb Box; right, #16273. 5" Aster Bowl. (65-85, 30-40)

7.58 - Black Satin Glass #329. 8 1/2" Lily Vases with gold decoration. (75-85 each)

7.59 - #9723. 10" Bud Vases: left, Black Satin Glass with gold bands; right, Ruby Satin Glass, undecorated. (100-150 each)

7.60 - Black Satin Glass: left, #9723. 10" undecorated Bud Vase; center, #9723. 10" decorated Bud Vase; right, #16270. 8 1/2" undecorated Bud Vase. (30-40, 45-65, 25-35)

7.61 - Reflex Green Satin Glass #9727. 10" Urn Vase, unknown gold encrustation. (60-80 each)

7.62 - Detail of Gold Encrusted Border (7.61).

7.63 - Opal #9727. 10" Urn Vase with gold decoration. (55-70)

7.64 - Lilac Satin Glass #9781. 10" Bud Vase. (rare)

7.65 - Rose Pink Satin Glass #9786. 6" Rose Bowl. (55-75)

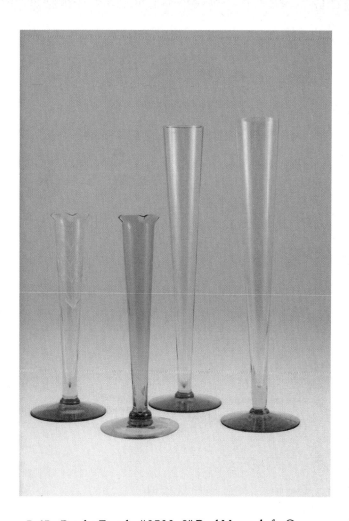

7.67 - Bright Finish #9723. 8" Bud Vases: left, Canary with Blue trim and light cutting; center left, Blue with Canary trim; center right and right, Bright Finish Canary with Blue trim #14185. 10" Bud Vases. (L 55-75, CL 45-55, CR & R 55-70)

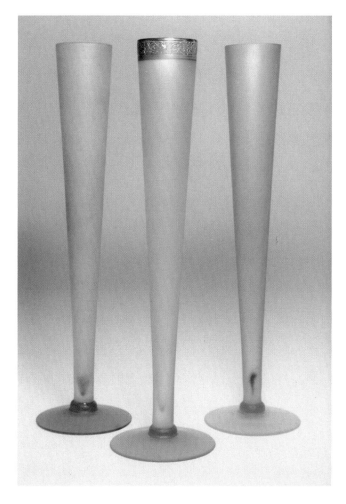

7.66 - Satin Glass #14185. 10" Bud Vase: left, Canary with Blue trim; center, Canary with Blue trim and encrusted MINTON Gold band; right, Blue with Canary trim. (65-85, 75-95, 60-80)

7.68 - Detail of MINTON Gold band (7.66).

7.69 - Opal #15319. 10" 2-Handled Vase. (175-200)

7.71 - Black #15319. 10" 2-Handled Vase with *SATIN RIBBON* Decoration. (140-175)

7.70 - Royal Blue #15319. 10" 2-Handled Vase. (125-160)

7.72 - McCourt Studios of Minneapolis, Minnesota, purchased a multitude of Black Satin Glass blanks for their *CORALENE* Decorated Lines: left, #16256. 5" *PEACOCK PRODUCTS* Poppy Vase; right, #16254. 6" *PEACOCK PRODUCTS* Iris Vase. (70-90, 85-115)

7.73 - Undecorated #16254. 6" Iris Vases in Crystal, Canary, and Black Satin Glass. (45-65 each)

7.74 - Undecorated #16254. 6" Iris Vases in Amber, Rose Pink, and Reflex Green Satin Glass. (45-65 each)

7.75 - For a brief period in the 1920s, a line of *opalescent ware* was publicized as "TIFFINware *with a Lalique finish,*" exemplified in this Sky Blue Satin Glass #16255. 8" Poppy Vase. (rare)

7.76 - Reflex Green Satin Glass #16244. 8" Poppy Vase with worn *CORALENE* Decoration. (95-125)

7.77 - Satin Glass #16255. 8"
Poppy Vases: left, Canary; right,
Sky Blue. (55-85, 45-75)

7.78 - Satin Glass #16255. 8"
Poppy Vases: left, Amber; right,
Reflex Green. (65-95, 55-85)

7.79 - Satin Glass #16255. 8"
Poppy Vases: left, Black; right,
Rose Pink. (40-65, 55-85)

7.80 - Black Satin Glass #16256. 5" Poppy Vase with *original* Bright Finish pierced flower arranger frog. (rare)

7.81 - Black Satin Glass #16256. 5" Poppy Vase, with Bright Finish pierced flower arranger frog removed (7.80).

7.82 - Ruby Satin Glass #16256. 5" Poppy Vase with *CORALENE* Decoration. Rare *color*. (250-325)

7.83 - The colorful enamels which adorn the blossoms and leaves of Tiffin's *embossed floral* lines are refracted through the small glass beads of the *CORALENE* Decoration, as seen in this #16256. 5" Black Satin Glass example with *blue* and *orange* flowers backed by *green* leaves and stems. (65-85)

7.84 - Black Satin Glass #16256. 5" Poppy Vases with *CORALENE* Decoration. (65-85 each)

7.85 - Undecorated #16256. 5"
Canary and Black Satin Glass
Poppy Vases. (45-60 each)

7.86 - Undecorated #16256. 5"
Reflex Green, Crystal, and Rose
Pink Satin Glass Poppy Vases.
(45-60 each)

7.87 - Sky Blue Bright Finish #66.
7 1/2" candleholders and #16256.
5" Poppy Vase. (Both 40-60)

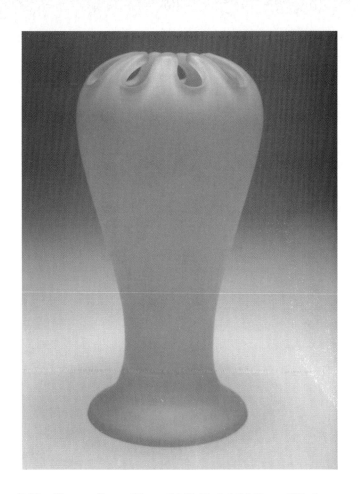

7.88 - Canary Satin Glass #16261. 8 1/2" Open Work Vase. This 'Open Work' style gives true expression to the term Flower Arranger. (50-75)

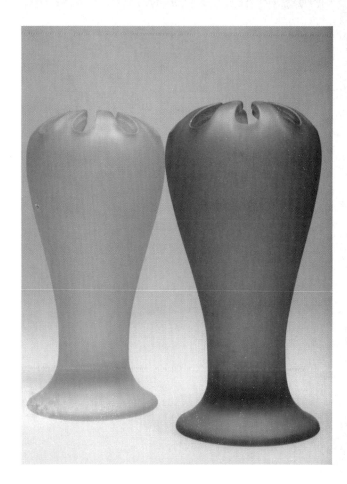

7.90 - Reflex Green and Emerald Green Satin Glass #16261. 8 1/2" Open Work Vases. (50-75 each)

7.89 - Sky Blue and Black Satin Glass #16261. 8 1/2" Open Work Vases. (50-75 each)

7.91 - Rose Pink and Amberina Satin Glass #16261. 8 1/2" Open Work Vases. (60-85 each)

7.94 - The textured pattern design of the mold is seen in these Reflex Green and Black Satin Glass #16264. 10" Vases. (65-90, 85-110)

7.92 - Amberina Satin Glass #16261. 8 1/2" Open Work Vase with gold decoration. (100-135)

7.93 - Black Satin Glass #16264. 10" Vase with McCourt Studio unusual *CORALENE* decoration highlighting the pattern design of the glass mold. (275-350)

7.95 - Black Satin Glass #16265. 9 1/2" TORCHIERE *Vase*, as identified in *China, Glass & Lamps*, February 11, 1927. (150-200)

7.97 - Black Satin Glass #16271. 10 1/2" Floral Vase with enamel decoration. (155-185)

7.96 - Crystal Satin Glass #16265. 9 1/2" TORCHIERE Vase. (110-150 each)

7.98 - Sky Blue Satin Glass #16273. 5" Aster Vase. (110-135)

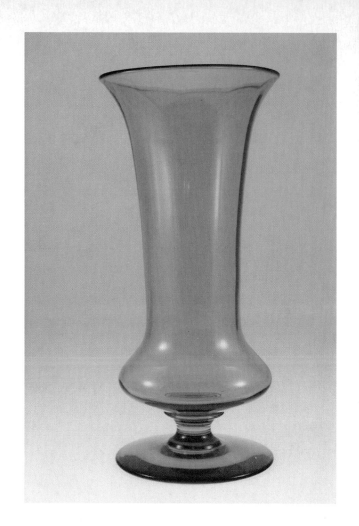

Opposite page;
Top left:
7.99 - Opal #17350. 9 1/2" Globe Vase. (185-225)

Bottom left:
7.100 - Unknown Line Number, attributed to Tiffin: Reflex Green Satin and Bright Finish 11 1/2" Vase with 'Venetian' decoration. (100-125)

Top right:
7.101 - Unknown Line Number, attributed to Tiffin: 12" Urn Vase, Blue with Canary trim. (145-185)

Bottom right:
7.102 - Unknown Line Number, attributed to Tiffin: Opal 9-3/4" Urn Vase with gold banding. (200-250)

Right:
7.103 - Unknown Line Number, attributed to Tiffin: Rose Pink Satin Glass 12" Cylinder Vase with enameled highlights on gold stencil decoration. (136-165)

7.104 - Unknown Line Number, attributed to Tiffin: Rose Pink Satin Glass 11 1/2" Vase with undocumented 'Rose Etching.' (110-135)

7.105 - Unknown Line Number, attributed to Tiffin: Blue Satin Glass and Reflex Green Satin Glass 11 1/2" Vases with undocumented 'Rose Etching.' (100-135 each)

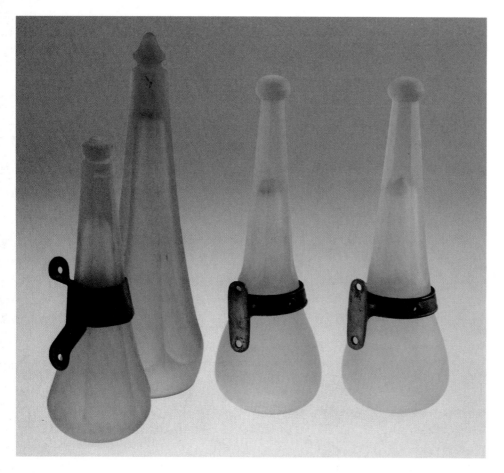

7.106 - The *Automobile Vase* is shown as a special type of Flower Arranger produced by Tiffin and sold with metal fittings necessary for easy installation: left, Canary Satin Glass unknown Line Number; left center, #16259. 8 1/2" Canary Satin Glass, shown without fittings; right center and right, pair Sky Blue Satin Glass with metal fittings, resembling Tiffin, but by Jeannette. (85 each)

7.107 - The #8127. 9 1/2" Bulb Box (7.52-7.57) was also available with a set of three "flower blocks" for use as a cut flower arranger. (*Crockery and Glass Journal*, June 3, 1926, p. 20. *Courtesy of Jones S.R.S. Archives*).

7.108 - The #8130. 5" Oval and #8131. 7 1/2" Oblong Bulb Boxes are seldom seen. (*Crockery and Glass Journal*, September 23, 1926, p. 2. *Courtesy of Jones S.R.S. Archives*).

Chapter Eight
GIFTWARE AND SPECIAL ORDERS

Imagine browsing through the aisles of a favorite department store or gift shop, shelves and counters stacked with TIFFINware, finding the perfect gift for everyone on your list: perfumes and atomizers for niece Nancy, candlesticks and candy boxes for Aunt Annie, a cigarette jar and ash trays for Uncle Bertie, book ends for husband Harry's office, a vase for Vera next door, and that new CRAQUELLE Lemonade Set for mom and dad. Better pick up a couple of items for 'High' and 'Low' at next week's Bridge Party, too...maybe some Satin Glass pieces. Boundless choices of giftware from Tiffin!

Additional Giftware and Special Order advertisements are shown at the end of this chapter, *courtesy of Jones S.R.S. Archives.*

8.1 - Rose Pink Satin Glass: left, *Milady* #331. 3 1/2" Powder Box (8.39); center, #8132. 6" Heart Bon Bon (3.8); right, #9305. Cigarette Box. (50-75, 95-115, 40-60)

Make Your Store
HEADQUARTERS FOR
Bridge Prizes
and Gifts of Glass

Popular Prizes that retail for less than $1

(Patent Applied for)

CIGARETTE JAR No. 9392

Fitted with vertical tray Crystal, black, sky-blue and apple-green—bright or satined.

SANDWICH TRAY No. 336

Wanted by every woman Rose-pink, apple-green, amber, canary and crystal, bright or satined.

(Patent Applied for)

REAMER SET No. 6456

Measuring pitcher fitted with detachable seed-catching reamer Pint or quart size—crystal or apple-green

BRIDGE SMOKER SET No. 9280

Makes a big hit. Each tray a different color—red, green, blue and yellow—all fired-in colors.

Colorful and Useful to retail for $1 to $2

(Patent Applied for)

SMOKERS' TRAY No. 9354

Ash tray, cigarette holder, two snuffers and match holder all in one unit. Apple-green, sky-blue and black—bright or satined.

FLOWER ARRANGER VASE No 16261

Very popular Rose-pink, apple-green, sky-blue or black—bright or satined.

(Patent Applied for)

GRILL PLATE No. 8861

Partitioned

Already in wide use for serving at receptions, bridge parties and afternoon teas. Crystal, amber, rose-pink and apple-green—bright or satined.

POPPY VASE No. 16256

A vase of rare beauty. Satined—with French Lalique decorations. In rose-pink, apple-green, sky-blue and rich black.

First Prize to retail for $2 to $3

OCTAGON SALAD SET No. 337

Four 8-inch salad plates of the very latest design. Rose-pink and apple-green. In individual cartons.

DANCING GIRL VANITY SET No. 9313

Puff-box and two colognes. In perfect taste. Rose-pink, apple-green, and sky-blue, satined.

CENTERPIECE SET No. 310

12-inch flower bowl—4 low candle holders. Satined rose-pink or apple-green. The present vogue.

(Patent Applied for)

Combination Iced Tea and Reamer Set No. 6450

Two-quart optic jug and cover with invertible reamer and six 12-oz. optic blown tumblers. Rose-pink, apple-green and crystal.

The items pictured on this page are a dozen of our best sellers. A window display of "Bridge Prizes and Gifts of Glass" will materially bolster up your summer sales.

World's Largest Makers of Household Glassware

SALES OFFICES IN ALL PRINCIPAL CITIES

Be sure to ask our salesman about the smart new OCTAGON Bridge Set No. 337, and the complete table service in this same much-wanted design—rose-pink and apple-green.

United States Glass Company, Pittsburgh, Pa.

8.2 -*Crockery and Glass Journal*, May 26, 1927, p. 6.

8.3 - *Milady* #331. 3 1/2" Powder Boxes: Ivory with gold trim (Rare); Canary Satin Glass (45-65); Sky Blue (50-75); Amber (45-65); Reflex Green (50-75); Black Satin Glass with enamel decoration (60-80).

8.4 - *Milady* #331. Dresser Set in Ivory with gold trim: pair 5-3/4" Colognes and 3 1/2" Powder Box. Rare.

8.6 - *Milady* #331. 4-piece Dresser Set in Reflex Green Satin Glass: 3 1/2" Powder Box, two 5-3/4" Perfumes, and 10" X 5-3/4" Tray. Original catalogs and trade paper advertisements sometimes identified the *Powder Box* as a *Puff* or *Rouge* Box. (200-250, set)

8.7 - *Milady* #331. Dresser Set in Rose Pink Satin. (200-250)

8.8 - Sky Blue Satin Glass: left, #9309. 4-3/4" Puff Box; right, #5764. 4-3/4" Cologne. (40-55, 65-85)

8.10 - Canary and Amberina Satin Glass #5768. 7 1/2" Colognes. (150-175, 175-200)

8.9 - #5766. 6-3/4" Cologne: unusual 'Dove Grey' painted Crystal blank with enamel decoration and gold trim. (85-115)

8.11 - Amberina #5768. 7 1/2" Colognes with Bright Finish. (140-165 each)

8.12 - Left, Sky Blue 5 1/2" Atomizer, unknown Line Number; right, #5768. 7 1/2" Emerald Green Cologne. (100-135, 125-150)

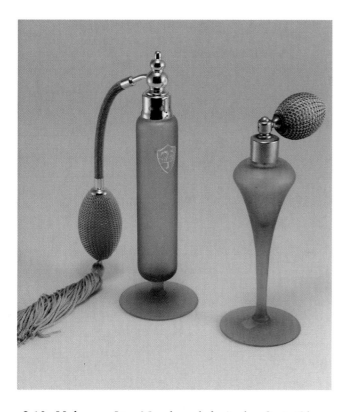

8.13 - Unknown Line Numbers: left, Amber Satin Glass 4 1/2" Atomizer; Sky Blue Satin Glass 4" Atomizer. (125-150, 140-165)

8.14 - Unknown Line Number: Black 5 1/2" Atomizer, *CLASSIC Etching* with Gold Encrustation. Rare

8.15 - Detail of *CLASSIC* Etching with Gold Encrustation (8.14).

#9313 DANCING GIRL

8.16 - Rose Pink Satin Glass #9313. 6" *Dancing Girl*
Puff Box. (150-175)

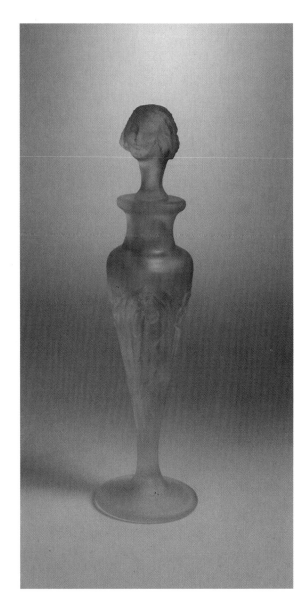

8.18 - Detail of #9313. 6-3/4" *Dancing Girl* Cologne (8.17).

8.17 - Rose Pink Satin Glass #9313. 6-3/4" *Dancing Girl* Cologne. The three side panels, showing a partially draped nude figure, are separated by three groupings of embossed daffodils. (200-250)

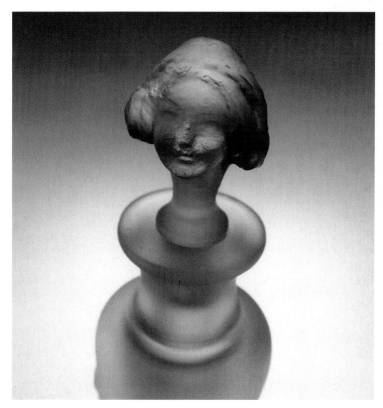

8.19 - Detail of #9313. *Dancing Girl* Cologne stopper (8.17).

GUILD GOSSAMER Line

Victor Hendrix (a.k.a. Hendryx) was a true Tiffin *Glassmaster*. In the late 1930s, he plied his skills as a craftsman in the production of the elusive and very collectible GUILD GOS-SAMER Line. Since, according to Mr. Webster, *gossamer* translates into '*gauzelike fabric*' or '*floating cobwebs*', this bubble acid *gossamer* treatment is aptly named! Difficult to explain, suffice to say it is not a *crackling* but, rather, an entrapment of actual bubbles *within the glass itself* ! Reportedly the sole artisan of this bubble acid process, a Line Number and the 'name' of this foreign-born *glassmaster* appear on every piece produced by him. This is not to say, how-ever, that it is *his* signature. Tiffin legend has it that, after immigrating to America, he never did learn to write and, further, was even un-able to sign his payroll checks. This may 'ex-plain' the '*y*' for '*i*' on certain pieces of *Guild Gossamer* . A glass cohort, schooled in pen-manship, was apparently enlisted to date and *signature* each piece for Mr. Hendrix.

8.21 - *Guild Gossamer* 12" Bowl and 12-3/4" ewer-shape Pitcher, both items signatured "Victor Hendryx." The Pitcher is further identified as Line "#177-8." (rare)

PARLOR and OFFICE

8.20 - *Guild Gossamer* Vase, H. 8 1/2", D. 10." Signa-tured "Victor Hendryx." (rare)

8.22 - Black Satin Glass #9298. 6" Ash Trays: left, made for "Carnegie National Bank"; right, "Stag Ash Tray." (45-65 each)

8.23 - Crystal #9352. 5 1/2" "Ship Book End" (8.51). (125-165 pair)

8.25   GUILD GOSSAMER 4-1/4" *Charlie McCarthy Hat,* signatured "Victor Hendryx." Charlie, of course, was a 'dummy' who, with Edgar Bergen as his partner, was a famous radio and TV personality from the 1930s to the 1950s. Production of this hat was reportedly limited to only seven pieces, one of which was presented to Charlie from the workers at Factory R. (rare)

8.24 - Amber Satin Glass #9352. 5 1/2" "Ship Book Ends." (100-150 pair)

8.26 - EISENHOWER *Vase,* signed "Duke Greiner," H. 10 1/2", D. 7." During his presidency, "Ike" was admired by the Glassmasters. Cut stars encircle the top rim of the vase and, at four points, also cascade down the sides, dividing the circumferential surface of the vase into four panels. The Presidential profile is framed in one while the 'White House Crest' adorns each of the other three panels. (rare)

"ROSES" Line

8.27 - *Roses* Satin Glass 10"
Candleholders, unknown Line
Number: "Green," Sky Blue, and
Canary. (125-175 pair)

8.28 - *Roses* Canary Satin Glass 4
1/2" Covered Puff Box with
enamel decoration. Unknown
Line Number. (75-100)

8.29 - *Roses* Canary Satin Glass: left, 7-3/4" Compote;
right, 6 1/2" Bud Vase. Unknown Line Numbers. (65-
85, 55-75)

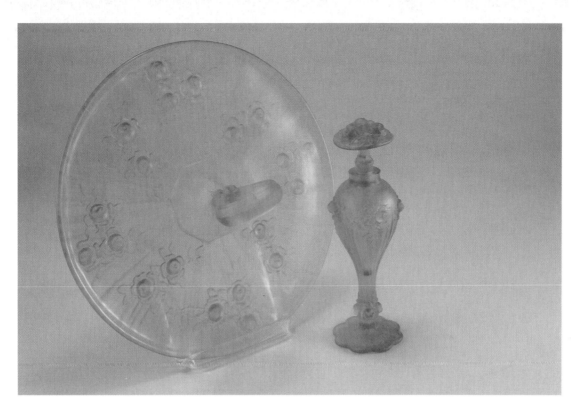

8.30 - *Roses* Sky Blue Satin Glass: left, 10" center handle Cake Plate; right, 7 1/2" Cologne. Unknown Line Numbers. (75-100, 135-175)

8.31 - *Roses* Sky Blue Satin Glass: left, 10" tri-footed Bowl; right, 11 1/2" Dresser Tray. Unknown Line Numbers. (55-85, 95-125)

SOUVENIR GLASS

Besides department store and gift shop buyers, owners of feed mills, general stores, and hatcheries also patronized Factory R. Their customers expected a gift or premium each year as a token of gratitude for the purchases they made during the previous months. Tiffin met the challenge with *personalized* or *localized* souvenir glass for these small businesses. The name of the 'store' or the 'town' will be found on colorful "Tiffin Glass" canoes, ash and pin trays, creamers and sugars, skillets, pipes, and bath tubs. Souvenir glass was a popular 'giftware' premium *back then* and is, for some, a popular collectible *today* . Decorated Souvenir Ware was pressed in Tiffin's deep production colors of the 1920s and 1930s as well as in Crystal, Opal, and Lux. Lux is a *clambroth white* non-opalescent translucent glass often used in globes and shades produced for lighting devices as well as in a line of utilitarian ware which Tiffin made for hospitals and dental clinics.

8.34 - Tiffin Souvenir Glass: Lux Glass ash tray, canoe, and knife, shown with Opal Glass skillet. (25-45 each)

SPECIAL ORDERS

8.35 - At the end of a production period, glassworkers were often allowed to use the 'end of a day's batch' to make items for themselves. The illustrated 13 1/2" Rose Pink Epergne, with Crystal *controlled bubble* connector, is reportedly such an item made at Factory R in the 1920s or 1930s. *Gerald Eakin collection.* Reader comments are welcome as research continues.

8-32 - Black Satin Glass 4 1/2" souvenir hat. (100-130)

8.33 - Emerald Green 6" souvenir pipe. (20-30)

8.36 - Rose Pink Miniatures, attributed to Victor Hendrix. All illustrated items approximately 2" H.

Additional trade journal advertisements, *courtesy of Jones S.R.S. Archives.*

S. S. MALOLO

The new flagship of the Matson line; American-Hawaiian Steamship Co.—owners. The Leviathan is also equipped with United States Glass Company ware.

8.37 - Tiffin enjoyed many profitable years supplying etched glassware to their institutional and commercial customers, including the American-Hawaiian Steamship Company (*Crockery and Glass Journal*, July 14, 1927, p. 5).

The entire glassware equipment— 40,000 pieces — of the largest and swiftest steamship ever built in the United States, was especially designed by the world's largest makers of household glassware.

UNITED STATES
Glass Company
PITTSBURGH

8.38 - Tiffin's Christmas 1924 advertising campaign featured more tableware than giftware (*Crockery and Glass Journal*, December 18, 1924, p. 94).

Dainty New Vanity Dresser Set

More For Milady

Made in Blue, Green, Canary and Amber.

No. 8851 Dresser Set

Organization

8.39 - *MILADY* was originally advertised as the #15331. Spiral Optic Dainty New Vanity Dresser Set (*Crockery and Glass Journal*, August 20, 1925, p. 5).

8.41 - Readers will note that *REFLEX GREEN* is the correct terminology for Tiffin's *light green*. This *name* was also listed in many of the Factory R production records and catalogs, as noted in the Goshe files (*Crockery and Glass Journal*, October 30, 1924, p. 11).

Above:
8.40 - *MILADY* was given a facelift in 1926 when a tray with the "base of the Puff Box moulded with it" was added to the set. Two rings on either side of the box stabilized the pair of perfumes, and the "new design" was also given a new Line Number, #8851. Few examples of this unusual dresser set are known (*Crockery and Glass Journal*, May 6, 1926, p. 33).

8.42 - Tiffin Cut Glass #5766. 1-oz. Colognes (*Crockery and Glass Journal*, May 1, 1924, p. 7).

8.43 - Decorated White Satin Glass Colognes. #5752. and #5762. are difficult to find (*Crockery and Glass Journal*, February 5, 1925, p. 10).

8.44 - The #9313. 6" *DANCING GIRL* Puff Box is easier to find than either the *ROSES* Toilet Water Bottle or the very elusive *Perfume Lamp* (*Crockery and Glass Journal*, February 2, 1924, p. 7).

A N ALL glass window display assortment adaptable also for counter and show case use. Made to accommodate practically all requirements by merely combining the different size units. Made from clear, polished glass. Assortment consists of the following units—

6 only— 3 inch male	4 only— 8 inch female
6 only— 6 inch male	3 only—10 inch male
6 only— 6 inch female	3 only—10 inch female
4 only— 8 inch male	6 only—Salver Top

One assortment per barrel.

UNITED STATES GLASS COMPANY
PITTSBURGH, PENNSYLVANIA
OFFICES IN ALL PRINCIPAL CITIES

Visit Our New Display and Sales Rooms—Pottery & Glass Bldg., 954 Liberty Ave., Pittsburgh, Pa.

8.45 - Tiffin manufactured all-glass "risers" for retail display shelving (*Crockery and Glass Journal*, August 21, 1924, p.7).

TWO NEW ITEMS
Typical of the diversified line of glass products manufactured by the world's largest maker of table glassware.

INEXPENSIVE VANITY SET

Two colognes and powder box in blue and amber for retail trade and in crystal for cutters and decorators. Will retail in colors for about $1. Order by No. 5764.

FOR ATTRACTIVE DISPLAY

Let us send you illustrations and prices on the now very complete line of adjustable glass display stands, showing all sizes and attachments.

UNITED STATES GLASS COMPANY
PITTSBURGH, PENNSYLVANIA
OFFICES IN ALL PRINCIPAL CITIES

Visit Our New Display and Sales Rooms—Pottery & Glass Bldg., 954 Liberty Ave., Pittsburgh, Pa.

8.46 - Left, the #5764. Powder Box is seldom found in the company of the matching Colognes; right, all-glass *shoe display* stands were added to Tiffin's assortment of display products in 1925 (*Crockery and Glass Journal*, September 24, 1925, p. 27).

8.47 - Fish bowls were important decorative accessories during the 1920s (*Crockery and Glass Journal,* December 24,1925, p. 27).

8.48 - Left, the #87. *PENDANT CANDLESTICK* has not been seen by members of the research panel; right, *FLOWER GARDEN WITH BUTTERFLIES,* as seen on the #15326. covered "Comport," was in production as early as 1925 (*Crockery and Glass Journal,* September 17, 1925, p. 5).

140

8.49 - Tiffin also catered to the Florist Trade, offering a #151. *Assortment* of flower bowls in 1924. (*Crockery and Glass Journal*, October 16, 1924, p. 9).

8.50 - Proof that *fish bowls* were popular decorative accessories is the mention that the #15151. 18" *Mammouth Bowl* (which was also available in a 10 1/2" diameter) "is large enough to accommodate a flower block in the center" and *"a couple of small gold fish"* (*Crockery and Glass Journal*, November 13, 1924, p. 10).

8.51 - A wide assortment of giftware was featured for 1926 (*Crockery and Glass Journal*, December 27, 1925, p. 37).

8.52 - Novelty Ash Trays were staple production items from Factory R (*Crockery and Glass Journal*, April 24, 1924, p. 7).

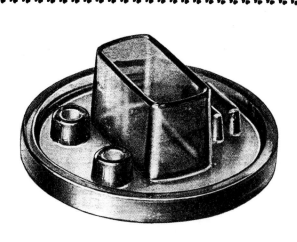
8.53 - The one-piece #9354. Combination Smoker's Tray (8.51) featured a container for an entire pack of cigarettes, a match box holder and two 'snuffers' (*Crockery and Glass Journal*, December 17, 1925, p. 187).

8.54 - In the 1920s, *cards* were a popular social pastime and Tiffin catered to the *players* in many of their advertisements. Individually boxed "Hostess Gift Sets" were available with two #310. 3 1/2" Favor Baskets and a pair of matching Ash Trays (*Crockery and Glass Journal*, June 18, 1925, p. 5).

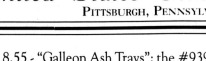

8.55 - "Galleon Ash Trays": the #9390. 6" style is seen less often than the #9389. 3" Ash Tray on the current collectible market (*Crockery and Glass Journal*, February 3, 1927, p. 33).

No. 6712 Night Cap Set

consists of a pint carafe and small tumbler, both pieces being paste-mould lime-blown glass, highly finished.

Most useful as a sick-room accessory, and for night service in the bed-room. The home worker enjoys it in the sewing-room, and the man of the family appreciates its convenience in library or den.

Made in crystal, light-green and rose-pink, transparent and with satined finish. Also decorated.

DECORATED 603

For the dealer there is a special assortment, made up of six sets satined crystal glass, decorated two each Nos. 601, 602 and 603, and six sets light-green satined glass, decorated two each "Parrot No. 14", "Forget-Me-Not" and "Red and Pink Poppy"—six of our most popular decorations—packed in a carton.

Decorators have found this number to be a big seller, using ideas furnished by their customers to meet specific needs. An ideal container for bath salts and other toileteries.

UNITED STATES GLASS COMPANY
PITTSBURGH, PA.

8.56 - Tiffin suggested their #6712. NIGHT CAP SET was also serviceable as an "ideal container for bath salts and other toiletries" (*Crockery and Glass Journal*, December 9, 1926, p. 42).

Little Bo-Peep Plate and Mug

Low priced items that find a ready sale. Interesting, educational and attractive. Handsomely decorated on heavy, substantial glass. Designed so that food is not easily pushed off the plate. Mothers and children both like them.

UNITED STATES GLASS COMPANY

General Offices and Salesrooms
South Ninth and Bingham Sts., Pittsburgh, Pa.

New York: 1107 Broadway
E. T. W. Craig, Representative
Philadelphia: 10th and Market Sts.
J. A. Hemple, Representative
San Francisco: 628 Mission Street
F. M. Dunn, Representative

Boston: 99 Bedford Street
M. A. Lovell, Representative
Los Angeles, 643 South Olive Street
J. F. Stirk, Representative
Dallas: Southland Hotel Building
D. D. Otstott, Inc., Representative

Baltimore: 110 Hopkins Place
John A. Dobson Co., Representative
Chicago: 30 East Randolph Street
F. T. Renshaw, Representative
Denver: 404 Jacobson Building
Norton C. Boyer, Representative

8.57 - The *LITTLE BO-PEEP* Set is the sole Tiffin advertisement for children's dishes on file in the Jones S.R.S. Archives (*Crockery and Glass Journal*, January 4, 1923, p. 8).

Chapter Nine
LAMPS

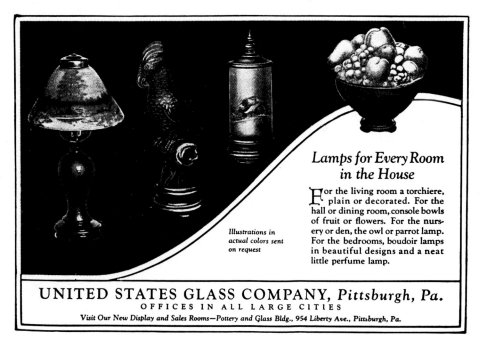

Lamps for Every Room in the House

For the living room a torchiere, plain or decorated. For the hall or dining room, console bowls of fruit or flowers. For the nursery or den, the owl or parrot lamp. For the bedrooms, boudoir lamps in beautiful designs and a neat little perfume lamp.

Illustrations in actual colors sent on request

UNITED STATES GLASS COMPANY, Pittsburgh, Pa.
OFFICES IN ALL LARGE CITIES
Visit Our New Display and Sales Rooms—Pottery and Glass Bldg., 954 Liberty Ave., Pittsburgh, Pa.

9.1 - *Crockery and Glass Journal*, February 14, 1924, p. 7. Tiffin Figural Lamps, unless otherwise stated, were decorated on Crystal blanks and sold with Bright Finish Black glass bases. An occasional example, however, such as the 11" Fruit Console Lamp (9.23), was sold with a fabricated metal base. Trade paper advertisements throughout this chapter are *Courtesy of Jones S.R.S. Archives.*

The Colonial Dame

Portable Lamp

A memory of Colonial days that blends harmoniously with the old four poster and the rag rugs of the boudoir of 1800. Gives a soft diffused light and serves admirably on dresser or bedside table. Hand decorated in soft tints—pink, green, and yellow. Base is lustrous black glass.

Lamp is complete with cord and plug in individual carton. No orders accepted for less than six.

UNITED STATES GLASS COMPANY
General Offices and Salesrooms
South Ninth and Bingham Sts., Pittsburgh, Pa.

New York: 1107 Broadway,
E. T. W. Craig, Representative
Philadelphia: 10th and Market Sts.
J. A. Hemple, Representative
San Francisco: 682 Mission Street,
F. M. Dunn, Representative

Boston: 99 Bedford Street.
M. A. Lovell, Representative
Los Angeles: 643 South Olive Street.
J. F. Stirk, Representative
Dallas: Southland Hotel Building.
D. D. Otstott, Inc., Representative
St. Louis: 1017 Olive Street. J. Donald Fisher, Representative

Baltimore: 110 Hopkins Place.
John A. Dobson Co., Representative
Chicago: 30 East Randolph Street.
F. T. Renshaw, Representative
Denver: 404 Jacobson Building,
Norton C. Boyer, Representative

9.2 - Tiffin's #E-3. 10" GIRL LAMP made her 1923 debut as *"THE COLONIAL DAME Portable Lamp"* (*Crockery and Glass Journal*, May 24, 1923, p. 8).

9.3 - Decorated #E-3. 10" Girl Lamp on Black Glass Base. (450-550)

9.4 - Opal #E-3. 10" Girl Lamp, undecorated. (450-550)

9.5 - 14" Large Parrot Lamp with blue enameled body, unknown Line Number. (800-1000)

9.6 - #E-6. 13 1/2" Parrot Lamp with red enameled body and an original 1933-1934 Century of Progress "Chicago World's Fair" label. Collectors of memorabilia from World's Fairs and Expositions place high values on unusual commemorative items such as the #E-6. Parrot Lamp. (400-475)

9.7 - Detail of Chicago World's Fair label (9.6).

9.8 - #E-6. 13 1/2" Parrot Lamps: left, orange enameled body; right, blue enameled body. (375-450, 325-400)

9.9 - #E-6. 13 1/2" Parrot Lamp with green enameled body. (350-425)

9.10 - #E-1. 8-3/4" Owl Lamps: left, decorated Opal;
right, decorated Crystal. (800-1000, 675-800)

9.11 -*Crockery and Glass Journal*, May 10, 1923, p. 10.

9.12 - #E-8. 8" Rabbit Lamp, enameled body. (1600-2000)

9.13 - #E-9. 10 1/2" Love Bird Lamp with blue enameled body. (450-600)

9.15 - #E-12. 8" Perfume Lamp with orange enameled body. (600-800)

9.14 - #E-9. 10 1/2" Love Bird Lamp with green enameled body. (450-600)

9.16 - #E-12. 8" Perfume Lamp with green enameled body. (600-800)

152

THE SANTA CLAUS LAMP

highly decorated — carries

Christmas Cheer into Store and Home

No. 7562
*Complete with socket,
cord and plug. Packed
in individual cartons—
six of these to a large
shipping container.*

Like a ray of sunshine through a rift in the clouds, this lamp will bring joy to the beholder. Its uses are many. It will augment retail store displays in show windows and interiors. From the retail trade there will be immediate response, as it is a novel home decorative number for the holiday season—under the Christmas tree or speaking its message of good will from hall or console table. Priced to retail at about $2.50.

UNITED STATES GLASS COMPANY
PITTSBURGH, PA.

9.17 -*China, Glass & Lamps*, October 14, 1926, p. 16.

9.18 - Decorated #7562. 10"
Santa Claus Lamp. (1800-2400)

9.19 - Decorated 13" Elk Lamp, unknown Line Number. (1600-2000)

154

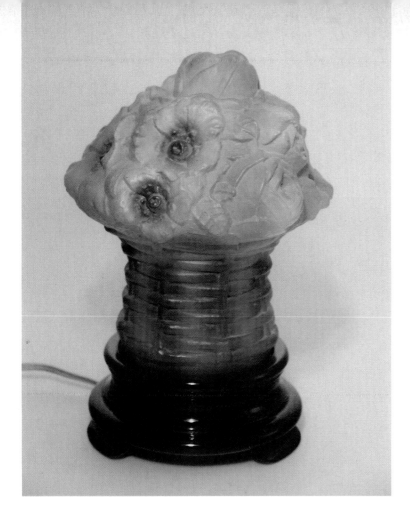

9.20 - #E-2. 8 1/2" decorated
Flower Basket Lamp. (500-700)

The Bouquet Lamp

A high class achievement in the glass maker's art.
This dainty bouquet lamp comes in the softest and
most delicate of pastel shades.   Its diffuse light
blends harmoniously with the furnishings of the
boudoir.   It can be used as a night light or bedside light, and it will make a charming table decoration for the dining room.

It comes packed in an individual carton, complete
with cord and plug and without lamp.   No orders
accepted for less than ½ dozen.

UNITED STATES GLASS COMPANY
General Offices and Salesrooms
South Ninth and Bingham Sts., Pittsburgh, Pa.

New York: 1107 Broadway.
E. T. W. Craig, Representative
Philadelphia: 10th and Market Sts.
J. A. Hemple, Representative
San Francisco: 682 Mission Street.
F. M. Dunn, Representative

Boston: 99 Bedford Street.
M. A. Lovell. Representative
Los Angeles: 643 South Olive Street.
J. F. Stirk, Representative
Dallas: Southland Hotel Building.
D. D. Otstott, Inc.. Representative
St. Louis: 1017 Olive Street. J. Donald Fisher. Representative

Baltimore: 110 Hopkins Place.
John A. Dobson Co., Representative
Chicago: 30 East Randolph Street.
F. T. Renshaw, Representative
Denver: 404 Jacobson Building.
Norton C. Boyer, Representative

9.21 - The #E-2. FLOWER BASKET LAMP was originally advertised as "The Bouquet Lamp" (*Crockery and
Glass Journal*, May 17, 1923, p. 8).

9.22 - #E-10. 8 1/2" decorated
Fruit Console Lamp. (600-800)

9.23 - Unknown Line Number:
11" decorated Fruit Console
Lamp with Figural Dolphin fabricated metal base. (700-900)

156

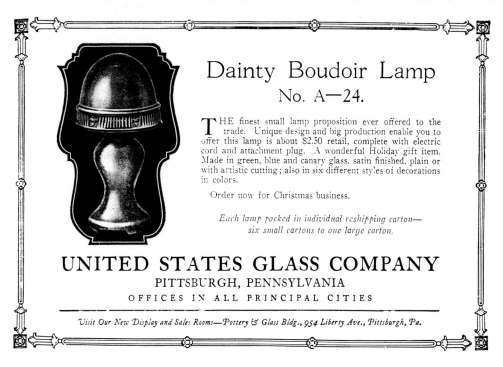
9.24 - *China, Glass Lamps,* November 19, 1925, p. 27. In January 1926, two months after introduction, the "No. A-24." Line Number was changed to "No. 7500." and advertised "in blue, green and canary, bright or satin finish with shade plain, cut in three artistic designs or decorated in color in floral or scenic effects, two pieces of glass with Edison base threaded collar molded in the glass standard" (*China, Glass Lamps,* January 18, 1926).

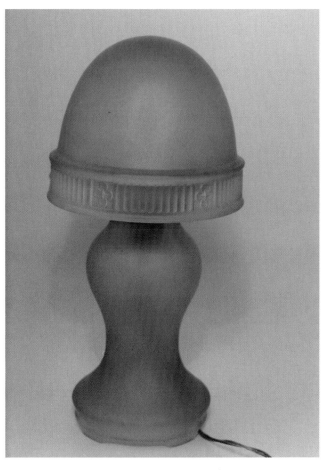

9.25 - Rose Pink Satin Glass #7500. 10" "Dainty Boudoir Lamp." (500-700)

9.26 - Canary Cut Satin Finish #7500. 10" "Dainty Boudoir Lamp." (575-775)

9.27 - Crystal Satin Glass #E-4. 10 1/2" "Torchere" Lamp with 'Owl' decoration. (375-550)

THE TORCHERE

An all glass lamp that meets every desire of the discriminating buyer. The torchere sheds a soft mellow light and harmonizes with the finest room furnishings. Can be used on living room table, mantlepiece and bookcases. Two decorations, one with all yellow shade, the other orange at the bottom blending out to yellow at the top.

Packed in individual cartons complete with cord and plug but without electric bulb.

Six cartons to a container. No orders accepted for less than one-half dozen of a kind.

UNITED STATES GLASS COMPANY

General Offices and Salesrooms
South Ninth and Bingham Sts., Pittsburgh, Pa.

New York: 1107 Broadway.
E. T. W. Craig, Representative
Philadelphia: 10th and Market Sts.,
J. A. Hemple, Representative
San Francisco: 682 Mission Street,
F. M. Dunn, Representative

Boston: 99 Bedford Street,
M. A. Lovell, Representative
Los Angeles: 613 South Olive Street,
J. F. Stirk, Representative
Dallas: Southland Hotel Building,
D. D. Otstott, Inc., Representative
St. Louis: 1017 Olive Street, J. Donald Fisher, Representative

Baltimore: 110 Hopkins Place.
John A. Dobson Co., Representative
Chicago: 30 East Randolph Street,
F. T. Renshaw, Representative
Denver: 404 Jacobson Building,
Norton C. Boyer, Representative

9.28 - Crockery and Glass Journal, May 3, 1923, p. 11.

9.29 - Crystal #E-4. 10 1/2" "Torchere Lamp" with Silver Overlay decoration. (425-600)

9.30 - Decorated Crystal #E-4. 10 1/2" "Torchere Lamp" with Black Glass cover and base. (425-600)

9.31 - The decorated #E-4. 10 1/2" "Torchere Lamp" was marketed in 1925 (*Crockery and Glass Journal*, June 25, 1925, p. 5).

9.32 -*Crockery and Glass Journal,* February 14, 1927, p. 27. Collectors will note the similarity of the #16265. "bas-relief" figure to the female form depicted on the panels of the #9313 *Dancing Girl Cologne* (8.18).

No. 16265
TORCHIERE LAMP
ROSE-PINK   GREEN   CRYSTAL
SATINED FINISH

The base and top are satin finished black glass, and the lamp is about 13" high.

The ornamentation is a graceful female figure, in bas-relief, repeated on each of the four panels, and the mitered corners, which are plain, add dignity to this charmingly decorative and useful household article.

The lamp is fitted with a 6-foot cord and two-piece plug, and may be equipped with a line switch, at small additional cost, if desired. Packed in individual cartons.

UNITED STATES GLASS COMPANY
PITTSBURGH, PA.
Sales Offices and Display Rooms in 18 Key Cities

9.33 - Crystal Satin Glass #16265. 13-3/4" Torchiere with *bright finish* Black Glass closure. (300-400) Collectors should be aware that 'reissues' of this item have been on the market since 1984 (*Tiffin Glass Collectors Club Newsletter*, Volume 10/No. 1 Spring 1995).

9.34 - Sky Blue Satin Glass #9664. 12" Electric Lamp Base. (300-450)

9.35 - Rose Pink #9730. 9 1/2" Water Lamp with Double Columbine-Variant Cutting. (325-400)

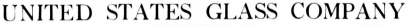

9.36 - *Crockery and Glass Journal*, July 8, 1926, p. 25

Introducing
The New Lamps

DEALERS everywhere are hailing these new lamps with enthusiastic delight. Bases are black, black decorated in gold, mottled blue and gold, and white. Shades are all hand decorated. The best looking low priced lamps on the market.

Ask for illustrations in color

UNITED STATES GLASS CO.
PITTSBURGH, PA.
OFFICES IN ALL PRINCIPAL CITIES

Visit Our New Display and Sales Rooms — Pottery and Glass Bldg., 954 Liberty Ave., Pittsburgh, Pa.

9.37 - *Crockery and Glass Journal*, March 27, 1924, p. 5.

They're New—

TWO new all-glass lamp bases make their initial appearance to please lamp buyers. The foot and top ring are black glass, the vase is decorated in brilliant colors,—blue, red, yellow and several others.

Each lamp is wired complete with six feet of silk covered cord and connection plug, all ready to receive the electric lamp and shade.

Furnished complete in reshipping cartons, six cartons to a case.

UNITED STATES GLASS COMPANY
PITTSBURGH, PENNSYLVANIA
OFFICES IN ALL PRINCIPAL CITIES

Visit Our New Display and Sales Rooms—Pottery & Glass Bldg., 954 Liberty Ave., Pittsburgh, Pa.

9.38 -*Crockery and Glass Journal*, March 19, 1925, p. 7.

Chapter Ten
POPULAR PATTERNS

10.1 -*Crockery and Glass Journal*, November, 1937, p. 1. The distinctive *VELVA LINE* is herewith added to the list of *Popular Patterns* produced at Factory R. Although long neglected by collectors of Tiffin Glass, *VELVA* continues to advance in popularity as an *Art Deco* collectible. Items from the *VELVA LINE* are shown at the close of this chapter.

CLASSIC Etching

10.2 - Crystal #23. 8" Vase with *CLASSIC* Etching. (225-275)

10.3 - Detail of the *CLASSIC* medallion (10.2).

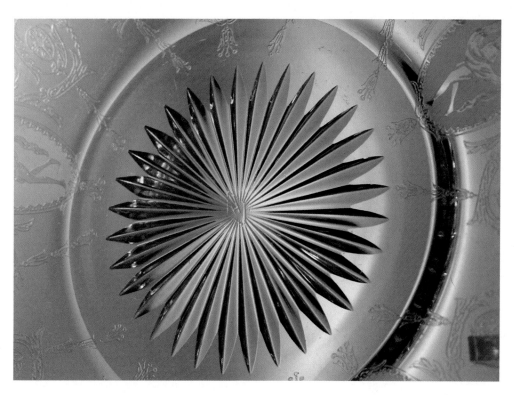

10.4 - A *CLASSIC* unsolved mystery is the presence of this Tiffin etching on *signed Heisey* Crystal salad plates. Reader comments are welcome.

10.5 - CLASSIC *Etching* on #024. Stem Line, Rose Pink with Crystal trim. Tiffin ads identified the #024. as a "shirred" stem: left and right, Champagnes; center, Wines. (35-40, 45-50)

10.7 - CLASSIC *Etching* on Crystal #15011. Stem Line with Nile Green trim. (45-55)

10.6 - CLASSIC *Etching* on Crystal #14285. drawn stems: footed Water; footed Juice; Goblet; Wine; footed Ice Tea; footed Whiskey; Sherbet. (Footed Tumblers, 25-40; Stemware, 35-55)

10.8 - CLASSIC Etching on Crystal #14185. Goblet and #114. "Tall Jug." (40-50, 225-300)

10.9 - Detail showing the overall design of the CLASSIC Etching.

10.10 - CLASSIC Etching on Crystal #14153. Grapefruit with Liner and #185. Parfait. (55-75, 40-50)

Encrusted CLASSIC ETCHING

10.11 - Detail of *CLASSIC Etching* with Gold Encrustation (8.14, 8.15).

10.12 - *Enamel Encrusted Etchings* were produced by The Morgantown Glass Works as well as by Tiffin, both companies using Crystal blanks with fired enamel trim. In this comparison photo, the Golden Iris (light amber glass) colored foot of Old Morgantown's #9704 Belton Luncheon Tumbler contrasts with the *green stained* disc-foot of Tiffin's #185. Table Tumbler: left, Morgantown *ROSAMONDE Etch* with 5-color encrustation; right, Tiffin *CLASSIC Etch* with 'garnet,' green, and gold encrustation (10.13). *CLASSIC* was also produced with a *green and gold encrustation* (10.14).

10.13 - CLASSIC *Etching* with Garnet, Green, and Gold Encrustation. (150-175 each)

10.14 - CLASSIC *Etching* with Green and Gold Encrustation. (140-160 each)

DEERWOOD Etching

10.17 - Detail of *DEERWOOD Etching* (10.15).

10.15 - *DEERWOOD Etching* on #2809. Rose Pink Goblet. Also produced on full line of #2809. Reflex Green stemware. (50-65)

10.16 - Detail of #2809. drawn stem and lower bowl (10.15).

10.18 - Detail of *DEERWOOD Etching* (10.15).

10.19 - Detail of *DEERWOOD Etching* (10.15).

10.20 - DEERWOOD Etching : rear, #196. Water Goblets in Crystal and Rose Pink; front, #2808. Reflex Green Table Tumbler and #185. Rose Pink 3 1/2" Sugar Bowl. (R - 40-50, 55-65; F - 25-35, 45-55)

10.21 - DEERWOOD Etching : rear: Reflex Green #330. 10" Handled Cake Plate and Rose Pink #8836. 6 1/2" Plate; front, Rose Pink #330. 10" Handled Cake Plate. (R - 85-105, 10-20; F - 100-130)

10.22 - DEERWOOD Etching : Reflex Green #330. 6 1/2" Whipped Cream and Reflex Green #151. 7" Sweet Pea Vase. (65-85, 80-100)

10.23 - Gold Encrusted *DEERWOOD Etching* : detail of drinking doe.

10.24 - #101. 5" Black Candleholder with Gold Encrusted *DEERWOOD Etching*. (150-180 pair)

10.25 - Gold Encrusted *DEERWOOD Etching* : Black Console Set: #8098. 11" Footed Orange Bowl with #101. 5" Candleholders. (130-160, 150-180 pair)

10.26 - Gold Encrusted *DEERWOOD Etching* : Black Cheese Plateau on 10" Cracker Plate with center indent and #179. Table Cream and Sugar Set. (185-225, 150-200)

10.27 - Gold Encrusted *DEERWOOD Etching* : detail of fleeing rabbit.

10.28 - Gold Encrusted *DEERWOOD Etching*: Black #15319. 10" Two Handled Vase and #15320. 7" High Foot "Comport." (175-225, 165-195)

FLANDERS Etching

10.29 - Detail of *FLANDERS Etching.*

10.30 - *FLANDERS Etching* on Crystal #15024. Line with shirred stem: Parfait, Sherbet, Goblet, Wine, Champagne, Cordial, Cocktail. (45-55, 20-25, 40-50, 45-55, 25-30, 50-60, 25-30)

10.31 - *FLANDERS Etching* : rear, Crystal #020. footed Ice Tea, Juice, Table and Whiskey Tumblers; front, Crystal #196. Oyster Cocktail. (R: 35-45, 30-40, 25-35, 30-40; F: 30-40)

10.32 - FLANDERS *Etching* on Rose Pink #15024. shirred stem Goblets with Green trim. (65-85 each)

10.33 - FLANDERS *Etching* on Mandarin Yellow with Crystal trim: left, #020. Juice Tumbler; center, #15024. Wine; right, #020. Table Tumbler. (35-40, 50-55, 35-40)

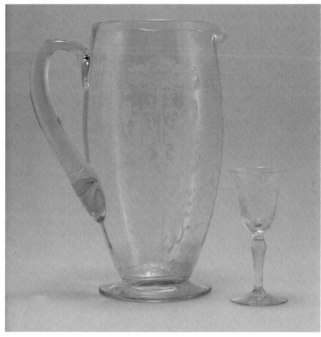

10.35 - FLANDERS *Etching* on Mandarin Yellow #194. 9 1/2" Jug and #15047. Cordial. (275-350, 50-65)

10.34 - FLANDERS *Etching* on Mandarin Yellow #5831. 8" Handled Plate and 4-3/4" Footed Bowl. (40-55, 50-65)

Opposite page, center right:
10.39 - FLANDERS *Etching* on Crystal #8153. 13" Centerpiece Bowl. (110-130)

Opposite page, bottom right:
10.40 - FLANDERS *Etching* on Mandarin Yellow #8153. 13" Centerpiece Bowl. (170-200)

10.38 - FLANDERS *Etching* on Rose Pink #179. 8-3/4" Conic Candy Jar with cover and #004-6. 5 1/2" Compote. (200-250 each)

10.36 - FLANDERS *Etching* on Crystal #15024. shirred stem Cocktail and #194. 9 1/2" Covered Jug. (25-30, 275-350)

10.37 - FLANDERS *Etching* on Crystal #583. 6" Compote. (60-80 each)

175

10.41 - FLANDERS *Etching* on Crystal Center Handled #330. 10" Cake Server. (140-160)

10.42 - FLANDERS *Etching* on Crystal #6. Table Sugar and Cream. (130-160)

10.43 - FLANDERS *Etching* on Crystal Cup and Saucer Sets: left, #5831. Line; right, #8869. Line. (35-45 each)

10.44 - FLANDERS *Etching* on Crystal 12" Hurricane Candles. (400-500 pair)

10.45 - FLANDERS *Etching* on Rose Pink #9758. 5" Candleholders. (225-300 pair)

10.46 - FLANDERS *Etching* on Crystal #5831. 6" 2-Lite Candelabrum. (145-165 pair)

FLOWER GARDEN WITH BUT-TERFLIES (#326. BROCADE)

Introduced as *BROCADE* in the 1925 trade journals, this Line is now called "FLOWER GARDEN WITH BUTTER-FLIES" (10.47-10.65). Most collectors are partial to items decorated with *MINTON Gold Encrusted Borders.*

10.47 - FLOWER GARDEN WITH BUTTERFLIES #326. Line: left, Amber 10" Center Handled Cake Plate; right, Emerald Green 7 1/2" Compote with cover. (65-85, 120-160)

10.48 - Detail of Butterfly on Sky Blue #326. 7 1/2" Conic Candy Jar (10.56).

10.49 - Detail of *MINTON Gold Encrusted Border* on Black #15179. 6" Covered Nasturtium Bowl (10.57).

10.50 - FLOWER GARDEN WITH BUTTERFLIES,
#326. Line in Rose Pink: 10" Center Handled Cake
Plate; 8" High Foot Compote. (80-100, 120-160)

10.51 - Detail of #326. Center Handle (10.50).

10.52 - Detail of a 'butterfly' and the 'garden' (10.50).

10.53 - FLOWER GARDEN WITH BUTTERFLIES
Reflex Green #326. 10" Low Foot Compote. (100-150)

10.55 - FLOWER GARDEN WITH BUTTERFLIES
Crystal #326. 7 1/2" Conic Candy Jar and cover. (95-130)

10.54 - FLOWER GARDEN WITH BUTTERFLIES:
Canary #326. 7 1/2" Conic Candy Jar and cover. (125-165)

10.56 - FLOWER GARDEN WITH BUTTERFLIES Sky Blue #326. 7 1/2" Conic Candy Jar and cover. (100-145)

10.57 - FLOWER GARDEN WITH BUTTERFLIES: top left, Emerald Green #326. 8" Plate; top right, Sky Blue #326. 8" Plate; bottom, Black #15179. 6" Covered Nasturtium Bowl on Black base. (20-25, 35-45, 175-225)

10.58 - FLOWER GARDEN WITH BUTTERFLIES #326. Line: left, Amber 4 1/2" Whipped Cream and ladle; right, Amber 6" Puff Box and cover. (70-90, 95-115)

10.59 - FLOWER GARDEN WITH BUTTERFLIES Sky Blue #326. 4 1/2" Whipped Cream. (75-100)

10.60 - FLOWER GARDEN WITH BUTTERFLIES
Sky Blue #326. 4 1/2" Whipped Cream and 8 1/2"
Candleholders. (75-100, 150-200)

10.61 - FLOWER GARDEN WITH BUTTERFLIES
Emerald Green #326. 8 1/2" Candleholders. (150-200)

10.62 - FLOWER GARDEN WITH BUTTERFLIES:
left, Black #151. 6" Cupped Dahlia Vase; right, Black
#79. 6" Candleholders. (150-225, 225-300)

10.63 - FLOWER GARDEN WITH BUTTERFLIES #15319. Line in Black: 10" Two Handled Vase and 8" Cupped Compote. (250-300, 150-200)

10.64 - FLOWER GARDEN WITH BUTTERFLIES Amber #326. Cheese and Cracker Set. (135-165)

10.65 - FLOWER GARDEN WITH BUTTERFLIES Black #15320. 10" Footed Cheese and Cracker Set, fitted with metal cover. (275-375)

10.66 - *Crockery and Glass Journal*, November, 1937, p. 1. Noting the Goblet and Sherbet, the *VELVA* Line was rightfully labeled as a Tiffin *"Table Service."* Although the factory Line Number is not known, the listing of satin finish as *"Frosty VELVA"* and the non-satin finish as *"Bright VELVA"* is an adequate reference for collectors of this *stunning* Table Service from Factory R.

10.67 - Regal Blue *Bright VELVA* 10" Two-Light Candelabrum. (225-300)

10.68 - Crystal *Frosty VELVA* 10" Two-Light Candelabrum. (175-250)

10.69 - Detail of *Frosty VELVA* Candelabrum (10.68).

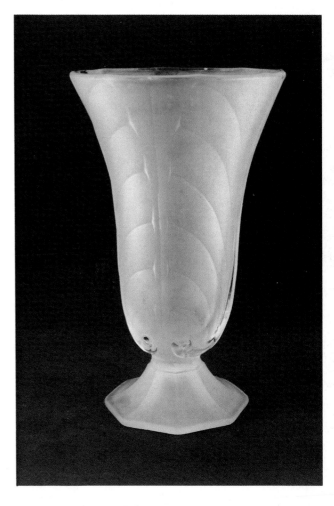

10.70 - Crystal *Frosty VELVA* 10 1/2" Vase. (130-160)

10.71 - Regal Blue *Bright VELVA* 4-3/4" Bowl and 6"
pair Candleholders. (45-65, 100-130)

10.72 - Regal Blue *Frosty VELVA* 11" Oval Bowl and
6" pair Candleholders. (85-115, 115-145)

10.73 - Regal Blue *Bright* VELVA 9 1/2" Fruit Bowl. (85-115)

10.75 - Detail of finial.

10.74 - Left, Regal Blue *Bright* VELVA 8-3/4" Footed Salver; right, Regal Blue *Frosty* VELVA two-handled 6" Bowl with Cover. (75-95, 115-135)

10.76 - Regal Blue *Bright* VELVA Table Sugar and Cream. (50-75 pair)

10.77 - Crystal *Frosty VELVA* : left, handled 6 1/2"
Two-Part Relish; right, Table Sugar and Cream. (40-
60, 60-85)

10.78 - Crystal *Frosty VELVA* 11"
Oval Bowl and 15" Oval Liner.
(85-115, 65-95)

10.79 - Crystal *Frosty VELVA* :
left, 8 1/2" Low Foot Compote
with unusual Platinum trim; right,
11-3/4" Five-Part Relish. (65-85
each)

BIBLIOGRAPHY

Although much of the material in this book was found in trade publications such as *China, Glass & Lamps* and *Crockery and Glass Journal* and in private archival sources, the following books are readily available.

Bickenheuser, Fred. *Tiffin Glassmasters, Book I.* Grove City, OH: Glassmasters Publications, 1979.

_____. *Tiffin Glassmasters, Book II, 1981.*

_____. *Tiffin Glassmasters, Book III, 1985.*

Florence, Gene. *Elegant Glassware of the Depression Era.* 6th Edition. Paducah, KY: Collector Books, 1995.

_____. *Collector's Encyclopedia of Depression Glass.* 12th Edition. Paducah, KY: Collector Books, 1995.

_____. *Very Rare Glassware of the Depression Years.* 4th Series. Paducah, KY: Collector Books, 1995.

_____. *Collectible Glassware from the 40s, 50s, 60s.* 3rd Edition. Paducah. KY: Collector Books, 1994.

Page, Bob and Dale Frederiksen. *Tiffin is Forever: A Stemware Identification Guide.* Greensboro, NC: Page-Frederiksen Publishing Company, 1994.

Tiffin Glass Collectors Club. *Tiffin Stemware.* Tiffin, OH: TGCC.

Weatherman, Hazel Marie. *Colored Glassware of the Depression Era, Book 2.* Ozark, MO: Weatherman Glassbooks.

INDEX

ABOUT THE AUTHORS

Leslie Piña has a doctorate in American Studies and is a professor at Ursuline College in Pepper Pike, Ohio. Her other books on glass include *Fifties Glass; Fostoria: Serving the American Table 1887-1986; Popular '50s and '60s Glass: Color Along the River;* and *Fostoria Designer George Sakier.*

Jerry Gallagher is a nationally-known authority on Old Morgantown glass, producer of *The Morgantown Newscaster*, and author of *A Handbook of Old Morgantown Glass*. He has specialized in American glass as a dealer and writer for many years and resides in Plainview, Minnesota.